THE FRANK AND ERNEST MANAGER

Jim Rosenzweig
Monty Kast
Terry Mitchell

Illustrations by
Bob Thaves

CRISP PUBLICATIONS, INC.
Los Altos, California
1991

THE FRANK AND ERNEST MANAGER

Jim Rosenzweig
Monty Kast
Terry Mitchell

CREDITS
Editor: **Michael Crisp**
Design and Composition: **Interface Studio**
Cover Design: **Carol Harris**
Cartoons: **Bob Thaves**

Copyright © 1991 by Crisp Publications, Inc.
Printed in the United States of America

Crisp books are distributed in Canada by Reid Publishing, Ltd., P.O. Box 7267, Oakville, Ontario, Canada L6J 6L6.

In Australia by Career Builders, P.O. Box 1051, Springwood, Brisbane, Queensland, Australia 4127.

And in New Zealand by Career Builders, P.O. Box 571, Manurewa, New Zealand.

Library of Congress Catalog Card Number 90-83480
Rosenzweig, Jim; Kast, Monty; Mitchell, Terry
Frank and Ernest Manager
ISBN 1-56052-077-9

ABOUT THIS BOOK

There are many excellent books available that introduce principles of management. Unfortunately, most are either too long (300 or more pages); too complex (inexperienced readers cannot apply the theory); or, more commonly, both. Professors Rosenzweig, Kast and Mitchell decided to attack these problems by developing this academically sound, yet invitingly readable book.

The Frank and Ernest Manager is faithful to the concept behind the best-selling *Fifty-Minute Book Series* that has made Crisp Publications famous. Although technically not in this series, *Frank and Ernest* reflects the same ''keep-it-simple'' philosophy and applied flavor of *Fifty-Minute* books. In many ways, *The Frank and Ernest Manager* provides an excellent overview of the topics covered by individual *Fifty-Minute* titles. A handy chart cross-referencing *Frank and Ernest* with specific *Fifty-Minute* books can be found on page 125.

We hope you enjoy exploring management through the adventures of *Frank and Ernest* and will continue to apply the management principles you learn long after this book has been read.

Have fun!

Michael G. Crisp

Michael G. Crisp
Publisher

ABOUT THE AUTHORS

It would be difficult to find three more qualified authors to write *The Frank and Ernest Manager* than Jim Rosenzweig, Monty Kast and Terry Mitchell. In addition to more than 90 years of combined college level management teaching experience, all regularly teach and consult in the private sector. They have written hundreds of books, articles and research papers.

Jim Rosenzweig is Professor of Management and Organization at the University of Washington. He holds numerous awards including being named Professor Exemplar. Jim is a member of Phi Beta Kappa, a Fellow of the Academy of Management and has served as Editor of the Academy of Management Review.

Monty Kast is Professor of Management and Organization at the University of Washington. He has served as President of the National Academy of Management and as Consulting Editor for IBM's publishing subsidiary Science Research Associates. Monty has presented seminars in numerous foreign countries on behalf of the U.S. Information Agency.

Terry Mitchell is the Edward Carlson Professor of Business Administration and Professor of Psychology at the University of Washington. He is a member of the Review Board of the Academy of Management Editorial/Review and the Journal of Applied Psychology. Terry is currently a member of the Governing Board of the Society for Organizational Behavior.

Jim, Monty and Terry believe that the cartoon characters, Frank and Ernest, serve as excellent examples to illustrate real world issues. All agree that theory that is not understood or cannot be applied is of no use. Frank and Ernest provide a fun way for readers to gain new insights about effective and ineffective behavior.

TABLE OF CONTENTS

(Continued on next page)

TABLE OF CONTENTS (Continued)

TO THE READER

We have followed the trials, tribulations, and exploits of Frank (the big guy) and Ernest (the little guy) in Bob Thaves' cartoon strip for many years. His cartoons provide a wide variety of humorous observations on the current American scene...situations and incidents that are familiar to us all. They provide a good laugh and a welcome relief from news reports, professional journals, and self-improvement articles.

For a number of years we maintained a separation of the humorous/enjoy aspects and the serious/endure aspects of life and work. Then it dawned on us: The ideas being communicated in cartoon format were relevant to understanding human behavior in work organizations—particularly caricatures of the behavior of ineffective managers.

We began to use the cartoon strips to illustrate key points in classroom discussions. Participants in management development programs seemed to enjoy them and they were able to identify with the characters depicted. ''That's the way it is in our company.'' ''That's exactly the way my boss does it.'' It was clear that the issues, concerns, and dilemmas faced by Frank and Ernest were typical of organizations, managers, and nonmanagers. Moreover, the appeal was international; cartoon illustrations were well-received in Australia, Singapore, Portugal, England, Hong Kong, India, New Zealand, Afghanistan, Indonesia, and the Peoples Republic of China. Students and managers laughed a lot and were able to relate the incidents to familiar local examples and thereby gain new insights about effective and ineffective behavior.

The idea for this book began to germinate—why not use Frank and Ernest to illustrate important concepts for understanding human behavior in work organizations? They could be ineffective examples (what doesn't work) and provide the stepping stones to guidelines for effective managerial behavior. The cartoons could serve as attention-getters. Then, once the reader is ''hooked,'' the discussion can proceed in such a way that relevant knowledge is applied to the dilemma presented. We would focus on a few well-founded (i.e., based on scientific research and sound theory) points that the reader can remember and apply in everyday situations, primarily at work.

TO THE READER (Continued)

We had trouble deciding on a format for the book. Frank and Ernest touch many diverse topics, thus providing an opportunity to organize in a variety of ways. We might have used tried and true managerial functions such as planning, organizing, and controlling, but this approach seemed deadly academic. We could have dealt with a series of miscellaneous managerial activities—goal setting, delegating, coaching, listening, negotiating, et al.—but this approach seemed too disjointed. We finally decided to use a relatively loose framework focused somewhat on an individual career cycle.

- Going to Work
- Work Organizations
- Doing the Work
- Relating to People
- Being a Manager
- Being a Leader
- Developing a Career
- Contemporary Conundrums

Everyone should be able to identify with these major themes. We get a job and work for others; we become supervisors and others work for us. We are followers and leaders simultaneously throughout most of our careers. We typically experience a variety of organization cultures and management styles during our working lives. We begin to discern effective and ineffective patterns of behavior. Frank and Ernest help us focus on some of the key issues and dilemmas involved in managing organizational behavior.

Frank and Ernest obviously point out the humorous side of work organizations. But this book is meant to be more than just a light touch. Our accompanying commentary is designed to be helpful and immediately applicable. Our view is that managers often take themselves too seriously. They could benefit by loosening up. Solemnity can be dysfunctional and may be ridiculous at times. We all need to recognize our foibles and be able to laugh at ourselves. Wholesome humor can be a liberating, relaxing, healthful, and powerful aid for effective managers. We see *The Frank and Ernest Manager* as a step in that direction.

Effective humor can trigger self-insight in a refreshingly pleasant way and thereby enhance learning. Cartoons can provide a basic message and stimulate learning through both cognitive and affective responses. (Jones, 1981, p. 10) ''The cartoon is 'communication to the quick' because it simplifies and exaggerates; it distills and distorts.'' (Harrison, 1981, p. 53) The message is concise and cogent; it is forcibly appealing to the mind. Incongruity and warped reality are attention getters. Readers typically project themselves into the situation depicted and identify with the characters. This is an important managerial skill. According to William Gould, executive vice president of the Association of Executive Search Consultants, ''What companies are seeking is someone who can see issues clearly. If a person can laugh, particularly at himself, he can probably step back and get the right perspective on things.'' (Kiechel, 1983, p. 205) Indeed, a sense of humor may become an increasingly important criterion in hiring and promotion decisions.

Humor can be an antidote to the stressors in modern organizations. It can reduce the anxiety caused by too much pressure or uncertainty. It can alleviate the boredom that comes with routine tasks and a sense of insignificance. It can defuse potentially explosive conflict situations. Laughter is relaxing and healthful to the body. It has been known to promote (at least facilitate) healing in stress related diseases. (Cousins, 1979) Note the term *dis*ease. Humor can put the mind and body at ease so that natural physiological processes can get back in sync.

The cartoons in this book can make a contribution to organizational well-being by encouraging participants to laugh at themselves. We make light of a powerful group—managers—who are striving to become professional.

Our aim is not to belittle or diminish what managers do. Rather, it is to help all of us understand that even serious activities can have a humorous side and that humor has an insightful message. We hope the cartoons in this book and the accompanying text illustrate the humor and document the important insights in an interesting and easy to read format.

PART

I

Going to Work

GOING TO WORK

Working is one of the most important of life's activities. Fortunately, most of us have a different view about work than Frank expresses in the cartoon on page 1. Although we all frequently complain about our jobs, particularly on Monday mornings, work is a fundamental part of human existence. Work has frustrating moments, but it also provides many of life's most significant joys and satisfactions.

Working is one of our most commonly shared experiences. Although there are some who are fortunate (or perhaps unfortunate) enough to be born into a leisure class, they are fairly rare in our society. It is the normal expectation that most people will work during most of their adult years. And contrary to Frank, many people like their work. There is substantial evidence that the work ethic is alive and flourishing; albeit in a somewhat mutated form from the past. Entrepreneurs, managers, and professionals seem to be strongly dedicated to their careers and willing to work very hard to accomplish goals. The growing number of women in the labor force and their movement up the ladder indicates that they are seeking and finding work satisfying and fulfilling. Almost all people, when given the opportunity for intellectual and emotional involvement in their job, display a strong work ethic. There is a decline in the desire for the mundane, repetitive, boring, dead-end jobs—we wonder if there ever was a strong desire for this type work. Maybe that's the kind of one-day job that Frank found so horrible.

The proportion of people employed between the ages of 18 and 65 has increased significantly over the past several decades. This is due primarily to the substantial number of women who have entered the labor force. These trends suggest that we are becoming a society with an increasing proportion of workers, typically employed by organizations. Although there are still a large number of family-owned farms and self-employed entrepreneurs, their proportions are decreasing. More and more we are working in organizations—with and for other people.

In *GOING TO WORK* we will look at various aspects of finding a job, joining an organization, and becoming an employee. Many of us vividly remember first going to work and the anxieties and frustrations when facing new and uncertain situations. Like Frank, many find the first day at work stressful and distasteful. But we kept with it and gradually things got better. At times we even enjoy our work. The following topics will be considered in this section:

- Recognize Me?:   Human Resources
- Trouble Shooter Wanted: Interviewing
- Frank's Inaptitude: Testing
- Have A Seat: Entering
- Noah Didn't Make the Rules Clear: Contracting

RECOGNIZE ME?: HUMAN RESOURCES

Individual people are the building blocks of work organizations. They go to work one at a time. All people are the same in some respects, but each individual is also different from every other human being. We have physical appearances and ways of thinking and behaving that make us unique. People recognize us not just by name, but by these unique characteristics. Other employees at the company's costume ball readily recognize Frank for what he is.

Throughout this book we will be looking at ways in which managers and employees think and behave in their working lives. A central theme is that peoples' behavior is jointly caused by their personal characteristics and the setting in which they find themselves. More specifically: *Behavior is a function of personality plus environment.*

What causes the uniqueness of each individual and what causes behavior have long been subjects of concern for philosophy, theology, anthropology, and psychology. Each of us has distinct characteristics or traits that lead to consistent patterns of behavior. We frequently refer to this ''something'' which represents the unique qualities of the individual, as personality. *An individual's personality is a relatively stable set of characteristics, tendencies, and temperaments that have been significantly formed by inheritance and by social, cultural, and environmental factors. This set of traits strongly influences the unique behavior of the individual.*

Certainly, heredity plays a great part. Physical and psychological characteristics are passed on from one generation to the next. There is increasing evidence that genetics plays an important role in alcoholism, responses to stress, and other behaviors. On the other hand, there is also strong evidence that life's experiences, particularly in the earlier years, have a strong impact on personality. Through the processes of learning and socialization we are shaped. The child who is raised in an abusive environment is more likely to become the abuser as an adult. Many of the so-called male and female stereotypic traits are learned through the process of early socialization. We can accept both viewpoints and agree that an individual's personality is the product both of inherited, genetic traits and of learning from experiences. Frank may have inherited the propensity to be an effective worker, but his life experiences have contributed to his becoming a slacker.

Once we reach adulthood, our personalities are largely formed. It is unlikely that we will undergo any fundamental change under normal conditions. However, even with a given personality our behavior may be quite different in various situations. Have you ever found yourself in a new and strange situation in which you were quiet and passive? Yet that same evening, when you were with a group of close friends, you were the life of the party. Same person but different situation; consequently, your behavior was quite different.

When we go to work, we bring the entire package to the organization—our genetic makeup and our learned ways of thinking and behaving. People have the unique capacity for thinking about their own attitudes and behavior and their impact on others—we have self-awareness. It is important to analyze our self-concepts in relationship to going to work. When the self-concept is compatible with the work requirements and job situation, the person is more likely to be motivated, oriented to high performance, and satisfied.

We have all heard comments like "people don't change" and "you can't teach an old dog new tricks." There is some truth in these ideas. Many factors within adults and in their situations cause resistance to change. However, we should not be confused by considering "personality" and "behavior" as the same thing. For the most part, when we think about people changing, we are thinking about their behavior, not their fundamental personality. People can learn new attitudes, skills, and ways of behaving in a particular situation. We start with a key premise that job success, including management success, is more a matter of developing skills rather than dependence on a particular personality type. Much of our behavior at work and in organizations is learned behavior. We learn a variety of technical, interpersonal, and managerial skills that help us function successfully. Frequently, these are skills and behaviors that we did not have before we joined an organization. Learning thus implies a basic change in our behavior. We are able to do something we could not do before. A worker can learn new skills in operating a machine or using a computer. As a manager, we can learn to be more effective in communicating, in negotiating, and in resolving conflicts. It is essential to be receptive to this learning in order to be successful in going to work.

Key Points to Remember

1. The basic human resource in work organizations is the individual—a unique personality.
2. Behavior is a function of the complex interaction between our personality and the situation.
3. For adults it is difficult to modify basic personality. However, it is possible to learn appropriate skills, attitudes, and work behaviors.
4. Accurate self-awareness helps in relating ourselves to work organizations.

TROUBLE SHOOTER WANTED: INTERVIEWING

Frank is taking a first step toward going to work; he is interviewing for a job. He is following good interviewing procedures by asking specific questions concerning the job duties. However, it sounds like wearing a bulletproof vest and being a trouble shooter may not be to his liking. Unfortunately, this may be one of the few jobs for which Frank is fully qualified.

The very thought of a job interview can intimidate people. Even more than the dentist, the surgeon, or the highway patrol, a job interview can bring on sleepless nights and daytime fears. Interviewing, for many people, is an anxiety-arousing, painful experience in which they display little skill or even common sense. It is part of a general job-hunting anxiety when most people feel insecure and vulnerable. It is difficult for the graduate interviewing for a full-time job. It can also be stressful for the older employee who is thrown back into the job market because of layoffs, or for a woman returning to work after raising a family. People feel a sense of not being in control of their lives and destinies; they are dependent on someone else to offer them a job. Many people feel uncomfortable when trying to sell any product or service. In the job interview we are trying to sell ourselves—a really challenging task. We fear rejection by others and the job interview most frequently results in this distasteful outcome. Successful job interviewing means managing this anxiety and then taking personal responsibility for the interviewing process.

The job interview should be thought of as a mutual exchange between mature adults; it is basically an interpersonal communications process. The primary purpose is the accurate exchange of information. It is not only desirable to communicate information effectively, it is also important to listen actively and to receive information accurately. It is not just the spoken word that counts, the non-verbal communications are equally important. Obviously, dress and personal appearance are the first things that the interviewer observes. Voice (tone, speed, volume), body posture, facial expressions, gestures, and eye contact all communicate information to the receiver. Evidence suggests that our impressions of other people are strongly influenced by these non-verbal communications and are often formed in the first few minutes of the interview. It is not just what we say, but how we say it.

The person applying for a professional, technical, or managerial position will frequently have not just one but several personal interviews. The initial or screening interview is used to establish the candidate's basic qualifications and to weed out obviously unqualified or uninterested applicants. The campus interview is typically a screening interview. The main goal is to pass the threshold and to be selected for the next important step. The second type of interview is with the person or persons who are actually responsible for the hiring decision. This interview is longer and the applicant can make the entire "sales presentation." A third type of interview is with people who may have some input into the hiring decision and may be working with you in the future. These interviews are likely to be more casual and their concern is "how will this person fit in around here."

The applicant should take substantial responsibility for the success of the job interviewing process. It is a mistake for the job hunter to act as if the responsibility for the success or failure of the interview is solely the interviewer's. What do we mean by the active management of the interviewing process? First, it is important to assess yourself, your experiences, goals, strengths and weaknesses. You are trying to sell yourself to the interviewer/organization and, like any top salesperson, the first step is knowing the product. The second step is knowing the customer—the job, the organization, the interviewer. Research indicates that applicants who exhibit knowledge about the firm and job requirements, who have specific career goals and plans, who ask pertinent job-related questions, and who appear articulate and poised are much more effective at influencing recruiters' decisions positively. The active management of the interviewing process also has an important secondary effect. It helps reduce anxiety. We feel more in control and less subject to the uncertainties of the situation.

The second side of the communication process is also important for the candidate—obtaining information concerning the company, jobs, peers, management, and organization culture. An important source of good, informal information is the company visit and interviews with current employees. They can give you first-hand information on what it is really like to work for the organization. People generally enjoy talking about themselves, their jobs, and careers. Frank obviously is in this stage of the process. He wants to know specifically whether or not live ammunition will be used in his job as trouble shooter.

Key Points to Remember

1. Most people are apprehensive about a job interview. This feeling is normal and is part of the general job-hunting anxiety.

2. Think of the job interview as a mutual exchange of information.

3. Non-verbal communications are particularly important.

4. The applicant should take responsibility for the success of the interview.

5. The overall goal is to provide information that helps the interviewer reach the decision that you are the best qualified person for the job.

FRANK'S INAPTITUDE: TESTING

Now that Frank has scraped by the screening interview for the job as trouble shooter at Acme, his next hurdle is passing the company's employment tests. Obviously, he is off to a bad start by filling out the wrong side of the aptitude test. The purpose of the aptitude test is to determine whether or not the job seeker possesses the potential for doing the job well. Frank may not measure up.

Next to the job interview, testing can cause the greatest concern for job applicants. Many of us suffer from test anxiety and can easily fantasize all sorts of horrible results. Understanding more about the objectives of testing, types of tests, and the application of results can reduce anxiety.

Employment tests are used as selection devices. With the "ideal" test the employer would be able to pick out the best, weed out the worst, and eliminate the necessity for engaging in other costly and time-consuming selection activities. Unfortunately, such perfect tests do not exist. Quite the contrary—there is evidence that some employment tests have only slight predictive validity i.e., the ability to predict performance on the job. This is the key issue in employee selection. It is not a question of how well the person does on the test. The issue is how well the person will do on the job. Good employment tests can be helpful in the selection process but they need to be used with caution and in conjunction with other screening procedures.

The use of tests to evaluate job applicants dates back to ancient Chinese bureaucracies. In the U.S., tests have been used extensively by military, government, and private organizations. Unfortunately, many of the early tests were questionable means of selection. The Civil Rights Act of 1964 and its enforcement by the Equal Employment Opportunity Commission challenged employers to prove the validity and relevance of their tests. This caused many organizations to abandon questionable testing procedures. Recently many new tests have been designed and validated and there is a resurgence of interest.

Four principle types of tests are used: achievement, aptitude, personality, and interest tests. Achievement tests sample and measure the applicant's knowledge and skills and demonstrate basic competence. Typing or computer operating tests are examples. Aptitude tests measure an applicant's capacity or potential for developing the skills necessary to perform the job well. Personality tests attempt to investigate dominant qualities and characteristics, such as intelligence, assertiveness, sociability, and decision-making style. Vocational interest tests seek information about an individual's interests, values, and preferences regarding various occupations. A company may use a battery of tests which includes all of these various types.

Some of the advantages of tests over other selection procedures are they have objectivity and are not prone to subjective interpretation. They are cost effective—an inexpensive way of screening prospective employees. On the other hand, there are disadvantages. Tests do not measure the strengths of motivation for job performance. Success on the job depends on both "can do" and "will do." Tests are more accurate at predicting failures than successes. They are generally better at screening out weak candidates than at predicting high performers. Tests may also be subject to dishonesty. Takers may try to beat the test by guessing what is wanted and giving socially acceptable responses. Tests may also create a high level of anxiety in certain individuals and therefore be poor predictors of performance.

In order to compensate for some of these weaknesses, a number of companies have established comprehensive assessment centers that use multiple methods to assess skills and traits of employees. They combine interviews, psychological tests, work samples, simulations, and group exercises into an integrated evaluation package. Most frequently, assessment centers are used to evaluate people already in the organization who have the potential to move into more advanced managerial positions. There is substantial research to suggest that assessment centers are effective in evaluating managerial potential. They also can provide an important means for coaching and career development. However, they are a costly means of selection. They also can create anxiety. Candidates who do well in the assessment center will likely carry a positive stereotype throughout their career. And candidates who do poorly may never be considered again.

Drug testing is a special form of employee testing which is receiving a great deal of attention and is very controversial. Drug problems in the workplace have become so critical that we are likely to see some form of mandatory testing used more frequently. Fortunately, there is little evidence to suggest that Frank has a drug problem. This is the one test he could pass with flying colors unless he drops the specimen bottle.

Key Points to Remember

1. There are various types of employment tests that attempt to measure different skills and characteristics.

2. It is normal to have test anxiety.

3. Tests deal only with potential. They cannot effectively measure motivation and effort on the job.

4. Test takers should answer questions as honestly as possible. If you try to slant your answers, many good tests will catch inconsistencies and your integrity will be called into question.

HAVE A SEAT: ENTERING

Johnson is facing a stressful situation. He is about to join an organization and he has already been given a difficult challenge. His new boss appears to take delight in making him uncomfortable. Johnson is engaged in the process of learning the ropes, more formally called *organizational socialization*.

The term socialization has nothing to do with political ideologies. *Socialization* refers to the process by which people acquire the knowledge, attitudes, skills, and behavior patterns that make them more or less able members of their society. We have all undergone this process many times. Significant socialization occurs during infancy and early childhood. We face resocialization on entering the first grade, joining an athletic team or the camp fire girls, going to college, and learning the ropes on our first job.

Organization socialization refers specifically to the process whereby the newcomer develops new values, attitudes, abilities, expected behaviors, and social knowledge appropriate for membership. Becoming an accepted member is a reciprocal process; the individual adapts, but so does the organization. Organizations are also subject to new influences that increase the likelihood of change. For example, opening up to greater participation by women and minorities not only results in the need to socialize these individuals, but also requires changes in the organizations themselves.

Successful organizations expend a good deal of effort to socialize their members. Companies such as IBM, Proctor and Gamble, and Microsoft have been highly successful in developing commitment on the part of individuals to organizational values. Commitment provides a means of self control. Many Japanese firms, such as Sony, Matsushita (Panasonic), and Toyota stress this process.

Effective organizational socialization can take many forms. However, there are some emerging patterns. Organizations that are successful in the socialization process and in obtaining employee commitment appear to (1) be careful in the selection process to ensure that candidates will fit into the organizational culture; (2) involve the newcomer in challenging tasks; (3) measure performance and provide timely feedback; (4) reward outstanding performance; (5) discipline members for violating corporate norms; (6) emphasize dominant corporate values; (7) communicate company stories, folklore, myths, and experiences; (8) provide appropriate role models; and (9) encourage the development of mentoring relationships.

Johnson is just getting started in this process. Obviously the boss is giving him a challenging assignment, but we don't know how it will turn out. The boss looks like he might give plenty of negative feedback, and would probably not be a good mentor or role model.

The initial period of employment—the first 3-6 months—appears to be one of the most significant times in the work careers of individuals. Newcomers are subject to many new influences. When they enter the organization they are uncertain about the roles that they will play. Finding themselves in stressful and uncertain situations, they are motivated to learn the ropes and fit in. They are more receptive to cues from the environment than they will ever be again and what they learn at the beginning will influence their motivation, job attitudes, performance, and satisfaction throughout their work lives.

Women and minorities have unique problems. They often have difficulty fitting into the dominate culture. More varied and heterogeneous human inputs into organizations require more adaptive and creative socialization processes. This is not only a process of change for the newcomers, but requires significant *resocialization* of existing members. This makes the process even more difficult.

Organizational socialization can be underdone, appropriately done, or overdone. If it is underdone it may lead to nonconformity, rebellion, and alienation on the part of the individual who rejects all the norms and values. The rebellious individual is dissatisfied with both himself and the organization. The other extreme is oversocialization where the individual totally conforms to the organization and unquestioningly perpetuates and demands acceptance of the status quo. The aim should be to develop creative individualism where the person generally accepts the key goals, values, and norms of the organization but also retains the desire to seek changes and improvements. It is vital for the organization to have diverse and creative human inputs in a dynamically changing world.

Key Points to Remember

1. Everyone undergoes a socialization process when joining a group or organization.
   It usually involves a period of uncertainty and stress.

2. Organizational socialization results in the individual developing new values and attitudes as well as learning new roles and ways of behaving.

3. Organizations with strong cultures spend a good deal of time and effort on the socialization process to ensure lasting commitment by employees.

4. Initial socialization is vital for individuals. They learn attitudes and behaviors that will significantly affect their careers.

5. Women and minorities have special problems in fitting into white, male-oriented organizational cultures.

6. The goal of organizational socialization is creative individualism where the person accepts the key goals and values but retains the desire to seek changes and improvement.

NOAH DIDN'T MAKE THE RULES CLEAR: CONTRACTING

What is expected of me when I join an organization? What do I expect from the organization? The mouse obviously didn't realize one of the most important expectations for joining Noah's Ark! Many people start working in organizations without very clear views of what they want out of their job or what the organization asks of them.

A basic part of the joining up process is the development of a *psychological contract* between the newcomer and the organization. This contract is not a written, legal document. Rather, it results from the process of reciprocation in fulfilling mutual expectations and satisfying mutual needs in the relationship between a person and the work organization. The psychological contract covers a wide range of expectations from the individual and the organization. The individual has expectations about what will be received over and above monetary compensation—satisfactory working conditions, career opportunities, challenging work, and fair treatment—as well as what must be given—time and energy, loyalty, willingness to accomplish organizational goals, and reasonable acceptance of authority. The organization in turn has expectations of what it will receive from the employee and what it will give in return.

The early phases of socialization involve sorting out and defining the terms of this contract. Not all expectations, neither the individual's nor the organization's, can be met; there is explicit and implicit bargaining in which each side has to compromise. The extent to which such bargaining is direct and open versus indirect and suppressed varies a great deal, depending on leadership style and organizational practices.

The development of a psychological contract is vitally important to the individual's long-term performance and satisfaction. There is strong evidence to suggest that the first year is one of the most significant periods in the work career of the individual. A number of research studies have found that employees given challenging initial jobs with high expectations for performance are more successful in their later careers than those given less challenging jobs. They developed a more effective psychological contract and were socialized to have higher aspirations and performance standards.

People have different expectations about their jobs and work organizations than in the past. Traditionally, monetary income and job security were most important. Gradually, employees developed expectations for having challenging and fulfilling jobs. Higher levels of education create greater expectations. Surveys of recent college graduates and current professional and managerial employees indicate that the key factor in job selection and job satisfaction appear to be intellectually stimulating work that provides an opportunity for advancement and challenging responsibilities. People are less tied to a specific organization and are more dedicated to their own career advancement. They will more readily change organizations to find the right career opportunities.

People are also striving to integrate their work and personal lives in a more harmonious manner. They are developing expectations that the organization will help in this process by providing day-care centers, leaves for meeting family responsibilities, opportunities for dual-career couples, guidance in financial planning, health, fitness, and recreational programs and many other personally-related activities. On the other hand, in helping the individual meet these expectations, work organizations are expecting greater commitment, increased responsibility, and more involvement by employees in meeting its objectives. There are always two sides to the psychological contract.

To ensure greater success during the organizational socialization process and a more effective matching of individuals and organizations it is important that each side make their terms (expectations) of the psychological contract more explicit. In too many cases, employees enter organizations with only a vague understanding of the situation and their own expectations. At times, organizations are also uncertain about their expectations. A number of organizations have attempted to provide prospective employees with more realistic job previews in the forms of booklets, films, visits to the work site, and informal discussions that convey not only the positive side of organizational life, but some of the potential problems and frustrations as well. The fears that this might put off the better candidates has proven unjustified, and research indicates that turnover and dissatisfaction are significantly lower for people who have received realistic information and expectations.

Key Points to Remember

1. Psychological contracts are formed between individuals and organizations that deal with expectations about contributions and rewards.

2. The development of an appropriate psychological contract would lead to good, long-term performance and a high level of job satisfaction.

3. Employee expectations are for challenging and fulfilling jobs that can be more effectively merged with their personal lives. Organizations want greater commitment in return.

4. It is important for both parties in the contract to make their expectations as explicit as possible in order to prevent unpleasant surprises.

5. Realistic job previews can help in the development of appropriate expectations.

Work Organizations

YOU'D BE GRUMPY, TOO, IF YOU WOKE UP AND FOUND YOURSELF AT WORK.

WORK ORGANIZATIONS

Does work have to be work? Maybe or maybe not, depending on our perspective. Work is physical or mental effort exerted to do something or to make something. It is also employment at a job. "Working" on your tennis game can be different from "going to work." For many of us, this latter concept of work can have a number of bad connotations—labor, toil, grind, etc., that lead to negative reactions like that shown at the left.

In primitive societies work is an integral part of living. Survival depends on hunting or growing or making whatever it takes to subsist. Specialization, bartering, manufacturing, and trading have made life more complex and led to separate work organizations—groups of people in joint endeavors with a common purpose.

In modern societies we have work organizations of all sizes, shapes, and degrees of complexity. They exist to produce a wide variety of goods and services. They grow and survive if they fulfill relevant societal needs. In large organizations, work is usually divided into functions such as accounting, marketing, and production. Differentiation by levels—front-line people, supervisors, executives—adds to the complexity. Thus, work can be experienced differently by individuals depending on the type of organization they are in and the particular job they hold. An engineering design manager may think about work significantly differently than a data entry clerk. Some people can't wait to retire; others dread retirement. Why? The main reasons are that people are different and jobs (work) are different.

Douglas McGregor set forth two polar views. Theory X: The average human being inherently dislikes work and will avoid it if possible. Theory Y: The expenditure of physical and mental effort in work is as natural as play. Most of us fall somewhere in between, depending on the particular kind of work. In general, digging ditches or waiting tables are not as much fun as playing baseball or singing. Even though the proportion of "drudge" jobs has decreased over the last 100 years, there still aren't enough pleasant, fun, glamorous jobs to go around. And most jobs may have both interesting and boring aspects. Thus, many of us may be stuck with jobs that turn out to be work (toil, labor, grind, etc.).

The specific task is one key to motivation—whatever it is that "causes" the expenditure of effort. If the work is intrinsically interesting and challenging, less attention needs to be paid to extrinsic incentives such as pay and fringe benefits. This has led to considerable attention to job enrichment as a means of improving performance and satisfaction.

On the other hand, not all work can be enriched. This view suggests that many of us work because we have to. How can we make the best of a potentially bad situation? Let's look at what it takes to survive, and even thrive, in work organizations by considering the following topics:

- Who Fits In?: Selection
- Tell It Like It Is: Orientation
- Magic Maxims: General Expectations
- Do What?: Roles and Tasks
- Form or Substance?: Rules of Conduct

WHO FITS IN?: SELECTION

"People hire and promote in their own image" is an adage that has a ring of truth. By and large, when managers are asked to list criteria and identify the qualities that are likely to lead to success at work, they describe themselves. It is only natural to project personal characteristics and behaviors into the selection process. If I've been successful, it stands to reason that people with similar values, beliefs, attitudes, knowledge, and skills will also be successful. But it is not always easy to find people who will fit into a specific work organization—as shown here.

Most organizations have gone beyond the "hire in your own image" approach. While they may still consciously strive to perpetuate a certain "culture," they are cognizant of the need to establish relevant criteria and make sure that all candidates are given thorough consideration and treated fairly. Affirmative action programs—legally mandated or self-imposed—have caused adjustments in selection behavior. Women and minorities at least have more of an opportunity to compete than was the case in the days when "good 'ol boy" networks prevailed. Changing behavior has resulted in changing attitudes.

In many organizations, diversity was avoided by screening out anyone who was different. If that approach didn't work, people were molded and shaped in order to eliminate or dampen differences. Now, at least in some cases, diversity is tolerated because it is required. But it takes enlightened managers to encourage diversity and celebrate its advantages. Of course, there are disadvantages. Things may not run as smoothly; there may be more conflict; and consensus may be more difficult to achieve. But more and different ideas can lead to creativity, innovation, and improved performance. Effective leaders are able to emphasize the positive aspects and cope with potential problems.

Individuals vary in the thoroughness of their search for the right job. Likewise, organizations can either pinpoint the right people in the hiring process or be less selective initially and then do a lot of "weeding out" during probation periods or the early stages of a career. Major accounting firms expect to "lose" 60 percent of their new hires along the way. Some organizations are committed to provide lifetime employment, but it is a difficult goal to achieve in our changing and "temporary" society. Even in Japan, where it is often cited as a major advantage, lifetime employment covers only about 25 percent of all employees. Regardless of expected turnover, voluntary or imposed, it is important to select competent people who fit and have the potential to succeed.

Lack of attention to the selection process can lead to grief for individuals and organizations. General criteria may be used because they are traditional and the process is comfortable, easy, and inexpensive. But an investment "up front" in fine tuning the process can pay off in the long run. This includes pinpointing specific job related skills and aptitudes to use in evaluating candidates. It means adhering to truth in advertising i.e., giving people a realistic view of what the organization is really like and what it expects from its members. Realistic job previews deemphasize the rhetoric that is often a part of the recruiting season, much like fraternity or sorority "rush" week. And it means encouraging candidates to make a thorough analysis by asking a lot of questions before they become committed.

An ongoing dilemma in many organizations is who should make selection decisions. Should the personnel department recruit, screen, and select new hires? Or, should it be the responsibility of line managers, or team members, or all of the above? The answer can vary with the culture of the organization, as well as its size, growth rate, and turnover experience. In small, stable organizations a manager can easily do whatever it takes to find and hire the needed people. In large, dynamic organizations the volume of hiring activity may make it impossible for a manager to do it all.

Whatever the approach, the key point is that the selection of new organization members is a crucial decision. Slipshod processes and poor choices can lead to time consuming remedial work and poor organizational performance. Systematic processes and enlightened choices provide resources that can maintain organizational well-being, and perhaps, encourage change and improvement.

Key Points to Remember

1. Be conscious of the human tendency to hire and promote people "in one's own image."
2. Recognize that the potential advantages of diversity can outweigh its probable initial discomforts.
3. Identify and use selection criteria that are relevant for success in specific jobs or career paths.
4. Make criteria and expectations clear so that candidates have a realistic picture that will improve the chances of a good person-organization "fit."
5. Invest time "up front" in a systematic, thorough, fair selection process in order to help prevent all the problems that stem from mismatches of people and organizations.

TELL IT LIKE IT IS: ORIENTATION

''They told me it could get 'hairy' at times, but I didn't expect it to be like this!'' How many times have you heard this or thought it? It is a common reaction because we often don't really know what we're getting into. Pre-employment or pre-assignment information tends to be sketchy. . .sometimes on purpose because we don't want people to know too much about onerous or dangerous tasks. With experience, Ernie should know that words like ''you'll like this job'' or ''this is a great opportunity for you'' can be ominous, especially when they are followed by change of pace words like ''but'' or ''except.''

It is human to be anxious in any new situation. This anxiety, coupled with the desire to make a good first impression, may cause us to stifle questions that we think are ''stupid.'' Orientation becomes a one-way communication process wherein we nod agreeably and mutter: ''Yeah, I understand.'' We don't clarify fuzzy instructions; we don't check for meaning; and we will be lucky to remember where the restroom is. This lays the groundwork for a rude awakening when it becomes obvious that we really don't know what is expected. How much better it would be if we could express our anxieties and engage in a two-way process of ''learning the ropes.'' This includes how to do the job, as well as information about co-workers, group norms, the boss's likes and dislikes, and company policies that are relevant for getting started.

From the organization's point of view, orientation of new workers is a crucial endeavor. It is important to make a good impression and get people started on the right foot. Lack of attention to the process can have lingering dysfunctional consequences. The ''here, read this'' approach can be deadly. The new hire is given a 400-page policy manual and told to study it. The ''sink or swim'' approach is the other extreme. The new person is thrown into the ''deep end'' of the job itself with the hope that he or she will survive and learn. The ''watch me'' approach is a middle ground that can be better if there is an opportunity to ask questions along the way and people are not ''kept on the sidelines'' for days or weeks.

The key to effective orientation is communication. The tendency is to error on the sparse side. Eddie Carlson called it NETMA (nobody ever tells me anything) when he was CEO of United Airlines. He worked hard at communicating on all levels and especially to new employees. What is this organization all about? What are its collective values, beliefs, and norms? What do we expect of organization members? This sort of general information sets the stage for specific expectations for people in particular jobs—pilots, cabin attendants, ticket agents, and baggage handlers.

Supervisors may have some anxieties when breaking in new employees that cause them to communicate ineffectively. They may assume that people are knowledgeable and hence not provide enough direction. Or, they may provide too much information to be absorbed readily by newcomers. In some cases too much help can be resented if people feel they already have enough information to perform effectively. The obvious answer is a happy medium—enough but not too much orientation. An ongoing two-way process should be helpful in determining the right amount for each individual. Asking for feedback ("How's it going?") will get the newcomer actively involved in the process.

A high-quality orientation process would serve the needs of individuals and the organization. It would relieve anxiety and make the individual as productive as possible as soon as possible. It would let people know what to expect and how to behave. The best approach is an interactive process that provides relevant information orally and/or in writing. But it would not be overwhelming. As quickly as possible there should be a trial run with ample time for questions and answers. In the early stages co-workers (autonomous work teams perhaps) or supervisors should keep in touch, but not hover. This allows the newcomer to ask for as much help as is needed. The weaning process can progress differentially according to the knowledge, skill, and aptitude of the particular person. Gradually a set of mutual expectations is developed that goes beyond the typical job description and allows the newcomer to become a comfortable and productive member of the work team.

Key Points to Remember

1. Try to relieve the anxiety that is normally involved in any strange situation like a new job.

2. Provide an appropriate amount—enough but not too much—information about the organization in general and the job in particular.

3. Get the person started doing something as quickly as possible without making her or him feel abandoned.

4. Provide as much help as is needed. Keep in touch but don't hover in a way that might indicate a lack of confidence.

5. Gradually develop a set of mutual expectations that goes beyond the typical job description to include personal relationships and group norms.

MAGIC MAXIMS:
GENERAL EXPECTATIONS

"As a man thinketh, so is he." This biblical adage brings up the issue of how values and attitudes affect behavior. Are the signs on Fenton's wall good indicators of his work habits? If so, our guess is that Frank and Ernie are about to throw in a few clichés of their own: "Failure is the path of least persistence." "Success is 10% inspiration and 90% perspiration." "When the going gets tough, the tough get going." At least it appears that they are a bit concerned with Fenton's easy going approach to work life.

Of course, the roles could be reversed. Fenton might espouse all the gung-ho, hellbent for leather, "win one for the gipper" slogans and become demotivated by the prevailing attitudes in his work group or upper-level management. He may be full of vim, vigor, and vitality...only to be dampened by bureaucratic rules and procedures. This suggests one reason—organizational constraints—why attitudes and intentions don't always translate directly into behavior.

Another reason is that it is easier to talk a good game than to play it. New Year's resolutions often go unfulfilled. Father Divine once lamented that he had a lot of theorizers in his church but few tangibilitators. Or, as Mark Twain put it: "To be good is noble. To tell other people how to be good is even nobler, and much less trouble." We judge *ourselves* according to our good intentions; we judge *others* according to their actual behavior.

Although general values and beliefs don't predict behavior very well, there is considerable evidence that they are related. The relationship is strongest when we compare specific attitudes and specific behavior. General acceptance of the so-called Protestant work ethic—a fair day's work for a fair day's pay—gives some indication of intentions. But specific positive attitudes about the organization and the job are more likely to translate directly into low absenteeism, punctuality, and reasonable effort. Of course, negative attitudes can lead to minimal effort and, perhaps, counterproductive behavior. Thus, organizations need to work hard on developing a generally accepted philosophy that includes specific guidelines for behavior.

Organizational culture is often captured in stories (sometimes apocryphal) or slogans or creeds that indicate the degree of emphasis in areas such as research, quality, customer relations, or teamwork. For example:

Toshiba	*"In touch with tomorrow"*
Honeywell	*"Together, we can find the answers"*
General Electric	*"Progress is our most important product"*
Bankers Trust	*"Excellence is achieved only through consistency and innovation...and teamwork"*
Motorola	*"Quality and productivity through employee participation in management"*

The general philosophies espoused in creeds such as these are apparent to everyone in the organization. However, they may not be internalized or put into practice by everyone all the time. The specific behavior required may be unclear or beyond an individual's capability. Quality service, teamwork, or progress may not be evident in every "encounter" with a flight attendant, loan officer, sales clerk, or account representative. The real culture is like the subsurface part of an iceberg—unseen but ever-present and formidable. We must live in a culture for a considerable period in order to experience the current effects of values, beliefs, and attitudes as they are demonstrated in day-to-day managerial and operational processes. Formal statements of intent can be helpful, but actual behavior is more important for understanding prevailing norms.

It is necessary to go beyond rhetoric and translate general slogans into explicit expectations for each role and then each person. If Fenton is a customer service representative, it is important for him to know exactly what is expected of him in that role—the norms. Frank and Earnest, the bosses in this scenario, need to set forth clear, challenging, realistic goals that get Fenton's attention and acceptance. If appropriate (legal, ethical, wholesome) procedures and behavior are important, they must be spelled out as well. The intention is that through a two-way negotiation process Fenton will become committed to a higher level of effort than is indicated by the philosophy evident on his wall.

Key Points to Remember

1. Strongly held values, beliefs, and attitudes can be good predictors of individual behavior.

2. Individual intentions to expend effort and perform well can be frustrated by organizational constraints.

3. Slogans and creeds are indicators of important goals and preferred behavior but they can be counterproductive if they are hollow platitudes.

4. Philosophical rhetoric should be translated into operational guidelines that can be used in all divisions and levels of the organization to enhance general commitment.

5. General guidelines should be translated into meaningful expectations for particular roles and specific individuals in order to elicit personal commitment.

DO WHAT?: ROLES AND TASKS

"All the world's a stage, and all the men and women merely players. They have their exits and their entrances; and one man in his time plays many parts." (William Shakespeare, *As You Like It*) Even Frank and Ernest remember this oft-quoted, nice-sounding bit of general philosophy from their high school English literature course. But, from the look on his face, Ernie is thinking: "Why do I get all the dirty jobs?!"

As the saying goes, we all "play" many roles—child, student, friend, spouse, teammate, engineer or accountant, subordinate, peer, boss, volunteer firefighter, and parent. How do we learn the scripts for these roles? Some may be built in genetically like the instinct for mothering. Others are picked up from role models such as parents, relatives, friends, teachers, coaches, fictional characters (TV, films, books, periodicals, etc.), elected officials, peers, and bosses.

Some roles like teacher or attorney or surgeon require specific knowledge about *what* the role entails and clinical experience in *how* it is carried out. Informal role models as well as "official" mentors have considerable effect on how a particular individual will behave in a specific role or profession or job. The ubiquitous television can be a particularly powerful source of models but there is no common theme.

In work organizations the job description is the formal means by which tasks are assigned to job holders. It sets forth minimum requirements in terms of obvious criteria such as knowledge, skill, and relevant experience. But job descriptions are often out of date even before they can be filed and forgotten. Changing circumstances and priorities call for revised procedures and new skills. And official descriptions can't cover everything...thus the typical last phrase concerning duties and responsibilities: "and anything else that comes up from time to time." It is unlikely that the job description for janitor includes anything about "cleaning up after livestock expositions."

In small firms, owner-managers are part or all of the work force. They often have to handle *everything* that comes up from time to time. Therefore, it doesn't make sense to formalize job descriptions. But as soon as there are two or more people involved, it does make sense to clarify the different roles and specify task assignments.

A disadvantage of formal job descriptions is that they can be used negatively; that is, they are used to delimit roles and jobs. We are all familiar with the frustrating and often dysfunctional response to a question or request: "It's not my job." Rigid, bureaucratic behavior may keep the organization neat and tidy, but it doesn't do much for customer service or teamwork. Excellence often means "doing whatever it takes" or "going the extra mile" in order to finish tasks and accomplish important goals. Enlightened managers put a lot of thought and effort into empowering people at all levels to "deliver" quality goods and services. This means pinpointing responsibility and authority so that individuals and work teams have the means to get the job done.

Roles and tasks can be fuzzy because of unclear or conflicting expectations. And overload occurs when expectations (from all directions) pile up and become impossible for one person to satisfy. A normally capable person finds it impossible to satisfy the demands of the job.

The foundation for effective performance is clarity of expectations that are current, challenging, consistent, and realistic. Within such a framework, the most appropriate behavior pattern for success is creative individualism, that is *not too far out of line*. Indeed, considerable training is designed to develop originality in problem solving, i.e., to encourage behavior that is uncommon but relevant within a defined organizational culture. The elements of success are judgment, timing, and style—doing the right things, at the right time, and in the right way.

Key Points to Remember

1. Most people "play" many roles in life, including their life at work.

2. Appropriate role behavior is learned in a variety of ways—emulation, education, and experience. Powerful, significant others such as parents, teachers, and bosses are particularly influential in shaping behavior.

3. Formal descriptions provide a first approximation to job requirements, but they should be augmented with continuing performance planning and evaluation discussions that keep expectations current and relevant.

4. It is important to check periodically for conflicting expectations (person-role, interrole, intersender, intrasender, and overload) that can be debilitating to anyone in a vulnerable position.

5. Be aware of the formal and informal expectations placed on you in a particular role, but forge a set of personal guidelines that communicates your capabilities and is heavily laced with your own values and beliefs.

FORM OR SUBSTANCE?: RULES OF CONDUCT

The personal policies of many school districts circa 1925 included words like these. "Women teachers are to dress and conduct themselves in a puritanical manner as follows: not to dress in bright colors; not to dye their hair; to wear at least two petticoats; not to wear dresses more than two inches above the ankle; not to use face powder, mascara, or paint the lips." It seems that Frank and Ernie (below) are concerned with appearance as well. Although Raunchmeyer is the fastest, most accurate mail deliverer in the district, he is not presentable enough—at least not in the daylight.

These are extreme views by modern standards. However, they do highlight the role of rules in controlling organizational behavior. Plans and procedures are means of guiding and coordinating the efforts of people toward common goals. Rules of conduct are detailed prescriptions and proscriptions that govern behavior. Certain basic requirements like attendance and punctuality are obvious in order to ensure that employees are available when work is to be done. But beyond the basics, how much is enough?

The Nordstrom employee handbook contains these two sentences. Rule #1: "Use your best judgment in all situations. There will be no additional rules." This approach is at the opposite end of the "control by rules" spectrum from the school districts described above. Most organizations cannot accept the existential view that "anything goes." The actions of a branch manager, department head, or supervisor must be legal and ethical. Some guidelines are made explicit by putting them in the form of written mission statements, creeds, policies, procedures, and codes of conduct. The "no additional rules" statement refers to *written* rules. There are plenty of ways of developing unwritten expectations or requirements for employee behavior.

Norms come to be understood by participants even though they are never written down. Employees are "conditioned" to certain behavior patterns through screening at the point of hiring, formal and informal orientation, and on-the-job experience. Nordstrom makes a point of letting department managers hire their own staff, thereby getting people with "the right stuff." Those that fit in thrive; those that don't leave. The survivors don't need a detailed set of rules to work by; they have internalized the norms of the organization. Management spends a great deal of time and effort in reinforcing the culture by exhortation, perpetuating myths and rituals, and acting as role models.

If the culture were strong enough—group value systems were internalized completely—all individual and organizational actions would fall within desirable limits and the system would be self-regulating. So far, however, this condition appears to be utopian, and considerable attention continues to be devoted to rules and their enforcement. But rules typically deal with minimal performance—what does it take to "get by" or escape punishment. They do not tap latent capability or encourage commitment or elicit performance "above and beyond the call of duty." Indeed, union members often signal a slow down by announcing that they will "work to the rules."

A significant issue in controlling organizational endeavor is deciding what is substantive for performance and what is superficial. For example, in our cartoon it doesn't appear that Raunchmeyer is "dressing for success." Should it matter? Values are changing with regard to this issue. Many nurses have given up starched white uniforms for more casual, colorful, and comfortable attire. At the same time, Safeco Insurance (1990) has reaffirmed its requirement of white shirts and ties for male employees. Partly it is tradition, but it may be seen as conservatism in a fiduciary relationship and therefore important in the eyes of customers. Moreover, there may be an assumed link with success. From almost any point of view, sloppy, dirty, unkempt servers in restaurants are about as popular as "hair in soup." Thus, there are times when rules about dress and hairstyle are important and functional.

The basic idea is that appearance standards, like all rules of conduct, should be relevant for the role and situation and make a difference in actual or perceived performance. Detailed regulations (mostly don'ts) about every aspect of a role or job can cause resentment and may be counterproductive.

Key Points to Remember

1. Rules of conduct are detailed prescriptions and proscriptions that are meant to govern behavior.

2. Managing via rules is the easy way to control behavior. A better way, but more difficult and time consuming, is continuing dialogue with subordinates that includes plenty of feedback concerning performance.

3. The stronger the organizational culture—internalized values, beliefs, and norms—the more management can rely on self-control, rather than rules.

4. It is wise to keep rules to a minimum. The "short list" should be clearly relevant for personal and organizational safety, health, and performance.

5. Involving employees in the development of rules is a good way to encourage "consent of the governed," a necessary ingredient for meaningful control of behavior.

PART

III

Doing the Work

MY PARENTS PLANTED
THE WORK ETHIC
IN MY MIND, BUT
I THINK MY BODY
REJECTED IT.

DOING THE WORK

Most people in industrial societies now spend part of their adult life working in an organization. The great majority of these people work full time jobs most of their adult life. That's a lot of people and a lot of time.

However, as the cartoon on page 29 recognizes, not everyone likes it or wants to do it. The word "work" after all is often contrasted with the idea of "fun." This suggests that there is something hard or onerous about work.

While that may be true for some people, the overwhelming evidence is that work can be a very positive force in our lives and most people prefer working to not working. Survey after survey conducted by major polling organizations (e.g., Harris, Yankelovitch) have consistently shown that 70% to 80% of employees are satisfied with their jobs. This percentage has changed very little over the last fifty years. These data lead us to two important questions: First, why do people work? Second, why do they work so hard?

We can answer the first question by saying "lots of reasons." The interesting point is that different people work for different reasons and the reasons for any given person change over time. Abraham Maslow recognized many years ago that work can fulfill people's needs for safety, security, status, affiliation, and achievement. Some, but certainly not all, of our reasons for working are focused on pay. Recognition is important; friends are important; feeling competent is important. And, as we grow older and more mature, these factors shift in their importance. But the central fact is that work provides meaning for our lives: goals, challenges, friendship, and support. While retirement may be something that many people talk about looking forward to, the fact is that unless other activities such as hobbies or volunteer work are available many retired people feel useless and bored and suffer psychologically and physically as a result. The work ethic is alive and well in the U.S.

The second question, about working hard, is related to our answer to the first question. Since people want different things and because their needs change over time, the key to encouraging hard work is to match organizational rewards with personal desires. Organizations are now starting to recognize that they need more flexible motivational systems. Cafeteria-style systems allow employees some discretion in the allocation of their remuneration. For example, they can make trade-offs between life insurance, pay, vacation time, stock options, or medical programs. Organizations are also emphasizing unique motivators such as day care, sabbaticals, work at home, flexible working hours, dental care, and counseling. These "extras" form a significant percentage of the total cost of employee compensation packages. Unions are also beginning to emphasize these issues in their negotiations so that there is a general recognition that more flexibility is needed.

As it turns out, our simple principle of matching rewards to people's needs is far more complex to put into operation than one first thinks. Management needs to be able to define clearly what one is rewarded for, set goals, provide feedback, monitor performance, and administer rewards in a timely fashion. We will develop these ideas further via the following topics:

- Reach the Unreachable Dream: Goal Setting
- Mindless Wonders: Task Strategies
- Setting the Stage: Motivation and Context
- The Carrot and the Stick: Rewards and Punishment
- The Devil Made Me Do It: Performance Problems

REACH THE UNREACHABLE DREAM: GOAL SETTING

The heart of the notion of motivation is striving: people wanting to work hard and to do well. But, different people strive for different things and in Frank's case the goal seems to be retirement—a goal which seems to run counter to notions of motivation and commitment to the job at hand. Everyone has goals; the important question is how management and employees can agree on goals that are mutually satisfying.

Actually, we know quite a lot about goal setting. We know that specific goals work better than general goals. It is better to tell the employee that 13 sales a month are expected than to simply say, "do your best." We also know that difficult goals result in greater motivation than easy goals. If 13 sales a month is average, then setting a goal of 15 a month is more likely to get higher sales than setting a goal of 13 a month. Obviously we cannot simply set outrageous goals—for goals to work they have to be seen as reasonable and they have to be accepted. But within these limits a tough goal works better.

The process of goal setting is also important. Setting goals jointly with the employee often enhances commitment to the goal. That is, if the employee participates in the setting of the goal, he or she is likely to have more of a sense of ownership of the goal. There should also be some built in buffers or renegotiation points. Unexpected things happen—priorities change, machinery breaks down, people get sick, and so on. Keeping the goal-setting process flexible is helpful and realistic. Finally, if possible, give some significant rewards for goal attainment—either in the form of recognition, money, or time off. If the flexibility exists, let the employee have some say in this process as well.

When doesn't goal setting work? Often, when people work in teams, it is hard to ferret out individual contributions—but in this case a group goal may be appropriate. When performance is hard to quantify it is also difficult to set goals. But in some cases certain *behavioral goals* can be set rather than performance goals. For example, one could concentrate on setting goals for the *number* of calls made, or the *amount* of information learned about the product rather than focusing on just sales.

The point is that goal setting, if done right, can be an important way to motivate people. It has been demonstrated in company after company and has become one of the standard practices of good management. Probably the most familiar place where it has been used is in Management by Objectives systems (MBO). These systems include long- and short-term goals as well as individual and group goals. It encourages participation in the goal setting process and flexibility for the revision of a goal. It is often part of a comprehensive appraisal and development system. If done right, it can be very effective.

Key Points to Remember

1. Specific, difficult goals, if accepted, are better than general or easy goals.

2. Participation in goal setting increases commitment to the goal.

3. Give rewards for goal attainment.

4. Whenever individual performance goals are hard to specify, use group goals or specify the desired behavior.

5. Make sure the goal setting program is flexible and negotiable—the unexpected frequently occurs.

MINDLESS WONDERS: TASK STRATEGIES

We really like this cartoon. As academics we are clearly supposed to think about things. Many times in our careers we have been sitting at our desks thinking (or even reclining in an easy chair) when a colleague or student has come by and said, ''Oh, I see you're not busy. Can I have a few minutes of your time?'' There is this automatic assumption that if you are not doing something that looks active then you are not working.

The truth of the matter is that a lot of jobs require complex thought processes. We think about problems, diagnose the situation for potential causes, think about solutions, weigh the alternatives using different criteria, and so on. Of course, a lot of what we do is, in fact, action. But a large portion of what we do requires thinking beforehand, if we want to do a good job.

We also need to be scanning the environment and thinking about the future. Much of what we do requires the correct anticipation of events. Accurate forecasts require the retrieval of information, processing what we know, and making contingency plans for various outcomes that may occur.

Obviously, the demands for these well-thought-out solutions vary as a function of job level and job type. The higher up one goes in an organization the more important thinking about planning strategies becomes. Top-level executives have to think about future directions and where they want the company to go. They make lots of decisions, many of which require reflection of some type or another.

The task at hand also makes a difference. More complex tasks require what is described as *task strategies*. People need to formulate plans about ways to accomplish tasks, what to do when things go wrong, and what sort of outcomes they anticipate. Task strategies have become an important topic for recent research.

For example, the goal-setting literature has been interested in task strategies. It turns out that as tasks become more complex, goal setting becomes more problematic as a motivational strategy. Goal setting has a much clearer impact on effort than task strategies. Specific, difficult goals clearly increase effort and on simple tasks that effort translates directly into increases in performance. However, on more complex tasks the effects of goal setting are less pronounced.

What these results suggest is that while goal setting may help somewhat on complex tasks, other techniques are needed as well. Task strategies can be learned through direct experience and the observation of others (e.g., modelling), as well as educational and training programs. Sometimes people use strategies from previous work that prove helpful (e.g., measure twice, cut once). In other cases they need to learn whole new ways of getting things done. For example, negotiation with a union may have similarities and differences to negotiations with competitors or the federal government. Using the wrong strategy in any of these contexts could have potentially devastating effects.

The points to be made here focus on both the supervisor and the employee. The former has to be aware that for lots of jobs, thinking on the front end turns out to generate benefits later on. For complex tasks such thinking should be encouraged and supported. Employees need to recognize that thinking is part of the job and that developing task strategies can be advantageous, especially on complex tasks. Trial and error learning coupled with the brute force of hard work is a costly way to proceed.

Key Points to Remember

1. Thinking is, in fact, working. It is to be encouraged and rewarded.

2. Doing the job right the first time saves time, energy, and materials.

3. High-level positions and complex tasks require well-designed strategies to improve effectiveness and efficiency.

4. Task strategies can be learned through experience, modelling, and training.

SETTING THE STAGE: MOTIVATION AND CONTEXT

Several messages are transmitted by this cartoon. At one level, we have an employee who knows a lot about the theory of motivation (because he has just written a report) but can't seem to put his knowledge to work—the secretaries won't type it up. As we all have experienced, knowing what we should do may be quite different from successfully executing our plans.

But a second message in the cartoon is more subtle and requires more discussion. Here we have a problem of performance (the production of a report on motivation) depends on it being written *and* being typed up. In other words, a successful outcome depends on the combined efforts of multiple contributors. To understand the importance of this point, we need to put the topic of motivation in perspective.

Motivation has to do with people wanting and trying to do a good job and the effort they exert to demonstrate that desire. There has to be some motivation for anything to get done. However, a manager or supervisor typically infers that a motivation problem exists because of a performance problem. More specifically, managers are alerted when projects aren't completed, deadlines are missed, sales or orders go down, supplies don't arrive, and so on. Their inference may well be "we'd be doing better if 'they' only worked a little harder."

The research suggests that this conclusion is often reached prematurely. More specifically, numerous factors contribute to performance problems and motivation is often a minor factor. So in order to determine whether motivation is indeed an issue, a number of other questions should be asked first. For example, the major determining factor for performance in most situations is the technology needed to get the job done. Machine downtime, computer malfunctions, poor quality or poor distribution of materials or information—these are the primary causes of performance problems. Before you worry about people working harder, make sure they have the information, tools, and equipment to do the job.

Even if the technical environment is very supportive and running smoothly, a second set of problems can limit performance. These are basically management issues: coordination, planning, and staffing. Most jobs require people to work together, share materials and information, co-ordinate their efforts, and have the right number of people available. The interdependence of the report writer and the typing pool is a good example illustrated in the cartoon. These people need to work together. Perhaps the secretaries won't type the report because they have too much many other things to do and they were not expecting the report. So a second place to look, before making a motivation diagnosis, is at the social mechanisms needed to complete the job.

If we still have a problem, should we infer that motivation is the cause? Probably not. It may be clear that the problem resides with one person or a group of people and not their work environment, technology, or dependence on others. But, there are still other factors that are more likely to be the cause of the performance problem. Of greatest importance is ability or skill. People may not be doing well because they don't have the necessary skills to do the job. For most tasks, it is clear that ability is the major personal determinant of performance. If the person is doing poorly, then perhaps training, education, or better placement is the answer.

Finally, when we have ruled out these other hypotheses, we can look at motivation and ask why the person isn't working hard enough? Perhaps they don't know what they are doing wrong. Perhaps they don't know how much they should be producing. Or perhaps they need help in knowing how and where to invest their effort.

The important point to recognize is that most performance problems are not motivational problems. They are much more complex than simply having lazy employees. But motivation can be an important contributor to effectiveness and we will discuss more specific prescriptions in the following units.

Key Points to Remember

1. Motivation is wanting and trying to do a good job. It is usually assessed in terms of effort: Effort that needs to be generated, directed, and sustained.

2. People usually think that a performance problem is due to lack of motivation but this inference is often premature or incorrect.

3. Find out first whether the technology, social context, and support activities are all running as they should.

4. If an individual or group does seem to be the problem, look for knowledge or skill deficits first.

5. Once you correctly conclude that motivation is the issue, you must match the correct motivational technique with the problem at hand.

THE CARROT AND THE STICK: REWARDS AND PUNISHMENT

We like to refer to the philosophy represented in this cartoon as the Darth Vader Theory of Motivation. Darth Vader, you will recall, was the evil instrument of the Empire in the Star Wars saga. He was the executive officer of the galaxy—spreading fear wherever he went. People did his bidding because they were afraid. When they inquired about the consequence of disobedience they were told: ''Prepare to meet your master.''

Organizations have motivational practices embedded in their history and their culture. You can tell when a place is engulfed by fear. It shows in the way people move, talk, and work. Threatened punishment is the means of motivation.

What exactly is punishment? In technical terms, it is the presentation or administration of adverse consequences following a behavior. Typically, a manual describes those actions and activities that are unacceptable. Accompanying these instructions are specific negative consequences that will occur if someone engages in these actions. These consequences are designed to hurt the person (financially, professionally, socially, psychologically). Pay may be docked, reports may be put in the performance file, the person may be publicly criticized, promotions may be blocked, and so on. Managers have an arsenal of punishments on which to draw.

Does it work? Well, if one means by that question does the behavior stop, the answer is usually yes. The conditions that accompany its effective use are as follows. First, the taboo actions must be well defined. Second, they must be known and understood by everyone. Third, the consequences must be meaningful to the person being punished. Fourth, the punishment must be applied regularly, immediately, and consistently—not just some of the time to some of the people. And, finally, people must know what the correct behaviors are to substitute for the incorrect ones. Things won't improve unless the correct set of actions are also well defined and rewarded.

While we readily admit that punishment works in changing behavior we would not recommend that it be the primary source of motivation. Fear is distracting. Punishment focuses on the negative—what people shouldn't do. Unfortunately, a far too common complaint is: "I only hear from my boss when I screw up." A climate of fear results in an uptight, uncreative, safety-seeking bunch of employees.

The research in this area suggests a positive system of motivation works better. People need to know what actions are valued and rewarded. Those activities also need to be well defined. They need to be rewarded (positive consequences occur) when they do things correctly. All too often, we fail to use praise because we expect people to perform well. The attitude of many managers is: "We pay them to perform well. Why should we have to praise them for it?"

People choose to do lots of things based on the consequences they think will occur as a result of their actions. A key managerial activity is the clear definition of what is wanted and expected. But an equally important activity is to use praise, recognition, social, and financial rewards frequently, consistently, and appropriately. While punishment is sometimes necessary, an overall system of motivation that focuses on the positive and rewards people for good behavior and desired results increases the probability of having a productive and satisfied work force.

Key Points to Remember

1. Punishment involves administering negative consequences for undesirable behavior and/or lack of desired results.

2. Punishment can change behavior if it is applied consistently, immediately, and regularly, and if the appropriate behaviors and results are known.

3. A climate of reward is usually more effective than a climate of punishment. People seem to work better if they focus on what they should be doing rather than worrying about what they shouldn't be doing.

4. Managers have lots of rewards they can use. Make sure you match the appropriate reward to the person and behavior in question.

THE DEVIL MADE ME DO IT: PERFORMANCE PROBLEMS

Unfortunately, this cartoon depicts a much too common phenomenon: the blaming of a subordinate for a performance problem. And in many cases, the same people seem to be singled out until they reach the not so elevated role of martyr or at least scapegoat.

Whenever something goes wrong, managers naturally try to diagnose the cause of the problem. They sort through information, think about the issue, draw some conclusions, and take some actions—usually punitive ones against a subordinate.

We know a lot about this process based on years of research. The manager is involved in a two step process: make a diagnosis and choose a response. The diagnosis seems to fall into one of two categories. First, there is a category that focuses on something about the individual employee—his or her effort, ability, or personality. The attributed cause (called an attribution) is *internal* to the subordinate—something about *them* that caused the problem. The second category consists of explanations that are *external* to the individual. Included here are lack of support, tasks that are too difficult, or unfortunate circumstances. These are environmental or situational attributions.

Once a diagnosis is made, the choice of an action, in most cases, follows fairly directly. Ability problems result in training or transfer; effort problems often lead to punishment or exhortations; tasks are changed when they are too tough; support is provided when needed; and counselling and sympathy follow bad luck. The response tends to match up well with the diagnosis.

However, a number of problems arise, both in making a diagnosis and selecting a response. Managers make errors that tend to be systematic. One of the most serious errors is that all of us tend to see the behavior of other people as caused by something internal to them (e.g., their character, effort, skills) rather than the environment. Yet the exact opposite is true when we explain our own behavior. People tend to see their own failures as contextually and situationally caused. This general bias tends to result in managers blaming subordinates for performance problems.

Another general bias is that we tend to see our *successes* as caused by us and our *failures* as caused by others or external forces. When subordinates succeed it tends to be seen as due to our great leadership, but when they fail it is their character that is the cause. When you combine both of these "biases" they result in subordinates frequently being blamed unfairly. This does not mean that they are never to blame—it simply means that when mistakes in judgment occur they occur more frequently in the direction of inappropriate scapegoating.

There are other biases that have been uncovered by research. People are punished less if they apologize for the problem. Managers make more external attributions for performance problems if the subordinate is someone they like, someone similar to them, or someone working at a job which they have worked at themselves. Also, if the outcome of an inappropriate behavior is serious (e.g., a nurse leaves a bed railing down and the patient falls out of bed and breaks a hip) the punishment is more severe than if the outcome is benign (e.g., the patient stays in bed). Even though the behavior is the same, the response is different. All of these biases create inequities, poor diagnoses, and inappropriate responses.

The solutions that seem to work best involve awareness, data gathering, and feedback. Managers should be made aware of the biases that easily and naturally influence their judgments. Training programs are available to help them in this area. Next, they should concentrate on gathering frequent performance data (e.g., weekly) on their subordinates. One recent study demonstrated that the use of a diary was helpful, with entries once a week. This information tells the supervisor whether the problem is unique to an individual (potential internal cause) or common to everyone (probably external); whether the person has been having trouble in this area for a long time (internal) or just recently (external); and whether someone is doing poorly at every task (internal) or just this particular task (external). Giving people summary reports of this type of information leads to the feedback being believed, accepted, and acted upon.

Key Points to Remember

1. Subordinates are often blamed inappropriately for performance problems.

2. Biases exist in the judgments made about potential causes and solutions selected. Biases caused by things such as apologies, or outcome severity, not only produce poor decisions, they also result in feelings of unequal treatment and discontent on the part of subordinates.

3. Supervisors need to be made aware of these biases and learn how to overcome them.

4. Keeping a performance diary increases the accuracy of managerial diagnoses as well as the acceptability of feedback.

PART

IV

Relating to People

RELATING TO PEOPLE

Most of what gets done in organizations gets done by people. While some highly technical jobs may not require personal interaction, most management jobs do. You have to get along to get along.

Apparently Bosworth's boss in the cartoon on page 43 doesn't particularly like the idea of relating to people. We suspect that many people feel like that, but having such an attitude is probably harmful for everyone involved. This section covers some important issues of dealing with people.

First, we will discuss what it means to be human. We will focus on the ways in which management theorists have described the basic nature of human beings and how these views influence organizational structure and culture. Included here is an emphasis on the uniqueness and individuality of each employee.

The second episode is about the communication process. Dealing with people well requires that we listen and speak and write effectively. To have good communications demands that the message gets sent and received, and that the meaning of the message is clear to both sender and receiver. Also discussed are the major blocks to effective communications and some techniques to increase its effectiveness.

Another key aspect of interpersonal relations is the process of participation and feedback. One of the major things that makes people satisfied with their work is the opportunity to contribute to the decision-making process. Requesting input from employees makes them feel involved and important. Of equal importance is communication from superiors to subordinates in the form of feedback. People need to know what they are doing right and what they are doing wrong. The former helps motivation and satisfaction, the latter helps learning and improvement.

The fourth issue discussed is creativity. It is defined as a process that results in new and innovative ideas, practices, and products. Techniques that encourage and facilitate it—such as brainstorming—are described.

Finally, there is the serious problem of discrimination. Dealing with different people requires that we treat them as individuals, not as stereotypes. More minorities, women, and older workers are in the work place and this heterogeneity can result in a dynamic and stimulating place to work. But it has to be developed, encouraged, and sustained through good interpersonal relationships.

We will develop these ideas further via the following topics:
- Merely Human: Being Human and Humane
- Say It Again, Sam: Effective Communication
- The Suggestion System: Participation and Feedback
- Eureka: Creativity Creation
- A Book and Its Cover: Discrimination

MERELY HUMAN: BEING HUMAN AND HUMANE

What does it mean to be human? If we work in an organization, we work with people. And this means we need to understand something about the human condition. Are there general statements we can make about which there is agreement?

THAT'S "ONLY HUMAN", NOT "MERELY HUMAN"!

© 1984 by NEA, Inc. THAVES 6-18

The cartoon seems to suggest that humans are flawed; that they are somehow not as effective or efficient as computers. In some ways this is probably true. But it doesn't present the whole picture. Our humanity is our uniqueness and there are some important aspects of being human that managers need to understand.

The early management theorists tended to have a fairly negative view of human nature. The Scientific Management approach viewed workers as basically lazy. The job of management was to watch employees closely to prevent loafing on the job. The stick was preferred to the carrot and the prevailing view was that employee behavior needed to be regulated and controlled.

In the 1930s and 1940s, the Human Relations school suggested a very different view of human nature. People were seen as basically wanting and needing to work and that work provided meaning for the lives. If given an interesting task and responsibility and incentive people would work hard on their own—because they wanted to.

The current view is somewhere in between. Most organizational experts see people as being capable of both conditions. The crucial factor, however, is not their genetic make-up but the environmental and social conditions in which they live and work. These ideas are widely held and have had major impacts on social policy and business practice.

The basic notion is that while all of us have our unique attributes, a lot of what we do is influenced by the setting and circumstances in which we find ourselves. People are strongly influenced by the people with whom they work and the expectations these people have of them. The feedback, rewards, and punishment that result from their actions are major determinants of behavior. Thus, organizations in general and management in particular can strongly influence what people do. People can and do change; their behavior can be modified. Humans are very malleable, given the right conditions.

But, as we've said, there is a unique contribution as well. Each individual has a specific genetic, social, and organizational history and this history influences how they react in particular situations. Some people want challenge and responsibility while others prefer security and certainty. Some people will always be on time while others may be early or late. Some will make deadlines, some will miss them. Some will be good oral communicators, others will prefer the written word.

The point about understanding this uniqueness is that *everyone* has things they are good at and not so good at. Everyone makes mistakes some of the time. For most people, the crucial task of management is not to ''shape them up or ship them out'' but to try to match job requirements and personal attributes. On the one hand, this requires a thorough understanding of jobs. But just as important is the need to understand people.

To gain this understanding requires some basic skills. You need tolerance to ascertain strengths and weaknesses. You need empathy to see things from their perspective. You need experience to understand what causes people to act the way they do.

How do you gain these skills? Ask questions. See what people think, want, and feel. Give feedback. Let them know what you think, want, and feel. Try not to judge immediately. Gather data first—a period of time, in different settings, and with various people. Don't assume that if a person has a performance problem that they are to blame. Look at the *whole* situation; the social and technological environment as well as the person.

In other words, understanding the human condition demands flexibility. People change, settings change, and a great deal can be done to help people be as effective as possible.

Key Points to Remember

1. People are neither inherently good or bad. They are a product of their genetic and social and environmental background.

2. The immediate social and technological context is a major determinant of behavior.

3. Humans are also unique and the proper match between person and context will result in the best performance.

4. Tolerance, empathy, and understanding are needed when dealing with others. Ask questions, listen, and give accurate, regular feedback.

SAY IT AGAIN, SAM: EFFECTIVE COMMUNICATION

Between 50 and 80 percent of a manager's time involves the transmission of information between people. This process is defined as interpersonal communication and it includes face-to-face discussions, memos, telephone calls, reports, letters, and any other process by which information is passed along or exchanged.

CAPSIZE?

6⅞.

THAVES 7-8

But, as the cartoon shows, lots of times we get it wrong. Poor communication has been blamed as the reason for the Watergate affair, the Exxon Valdez oil spill, the Chernobyl nuclear disaster, the Iran-Contra affair, and the Challenger disaster. In many cases the information that would have led to an accurate assessment of these events was available. However, it was evaluated incorrectly or not brought to the attention of the right people.

Effective communication involves more than just having the right information. The information must be believed, weighted correctly, reach the right decision makers at the right time, and result in an appropriate action. It is a highly complex process.

And the obstacles for effective communication are numerous. First, there is often a break in the communication link. Because of the size and complexity of many organizations it is often very frustrating to try to get a message to another person. Mail gets lost, phone messages get discarded, or an intermediary fails to pass information along. In many cases, person A simply forgets or doesn't try to get the information along to person B. It is very frustrating indeed.

A second problem occurs when there is some sort of distortion along the way from A to B. In many cases large amounts of information are condensed into executive summaries. Not only does this process involve selectively choosing what to say, it also involves what we call "uncertainty absorption." One frequently makes the message sound more certain and specific as well as more positive when it is passed along, than when it was received.

But even if the message gets through intact to person B, there can still be a problem. As the cartoon shows, the recipient may have a different frame of reference or ascribe different meaning to the information than was intended by the sender. People hear what they want to hear, or what they expect to hear. They look at who is sending the message and interpret its meaning accordingly. Speakers often use very subtle nonverbal cues when talking to someone.

And, finally, the sender and receiver are within a certain context. They may be incredibly overloaded with information. They may work in an organization where no one trusts anyone else. The technology for communicating (e.g., phones, memos, computers) may be unreliable. As we have said, there are lots of ways to go wrong.

But there are some things we can do right. First, we can build checks in the system to make sure messages are sent or received. People can tick their name off a list, phone to a central number, or utilize personal acknowledgments upon receipt of information. The Kai Tak Airport Manager inserted a space in the middle of a weekly report that was routed among the staff. ''Initial if you read this far.'' No one initialed it! We can also use multiple means for sending or recording information. Follow up a phone call with an announcement on a bulletin board or a memo. Keep minutes of or tape record the interactions and decisions in a meeting. Whenever possible, make sure that communication is a two-way process and that the recipient has to respond. And, make sure that everyone who might need the information is included. It is far better to err in the direction of openness than secrecy.

Second, the sender of information should always attempt to use language that is clear, concise, and appropriate for the setting. Think twice, go over the message one more time, and put yourself in the place of your audience. Try to avoid the use of labels, jargon, or language that can be misinterpreted.

Third, there are courses available to train people to speak more clearly and forcefully, to read faster with greater comprehension, and to be better listeners. Repeat what people have said to make sure you have heard it correctly. Summarize what you've heard. Pay attention to all the cues—verbal and nonverbal. Give *your* impression of the meaning of the message. All these techniques can help ensure that you have interpreted something correctly. Effective communication is critical in human organizations; and any investment in improving it will be time and money well spent.

Key Points to Remember

1. Communication is important. It takes up much of our time and is often the cause of major organizational problems.

2. Effective communication means that the recipient actually gets the message that was intended and sent, then interprets it the way the sender meant it to be interpreted.

3. Blocks to effective communication include a breakdown in the linkage, distortion along the line, or distortion by the recipient.

4. Using multiple checks in the system; learning how to send and receive messages and building an environment of trust and openness can help make communication more effective.

THE SUGGESTION SYSTEM: PARTICIPATION AND FEEDBACK

Two months ago Arthur Higgerty attended a management development workshop on the benefits of employee participation. He was a bit skeptical of allowing *his* people to make suggestions about how to do the work. But he was willing to try it. He had been persuaded by the promise of improved performance and morale—the benefits emphasized by the workshop leaders, both of whom were highly regarded consultants. They suggested that Arthur and the other managers encourage feedback from their subordinates, including ideas for improvements in the way things were done.

Arthur tried. He announced his intentions and formally inaugurated a Suggestion System to be run by the personnel department. A number of suggestions were dismissed by the Review Committee as "silly." Some people were chided for complaining about the organization or its managers. In many cases, employees received no feedback concerning what happened to their suggestions. Had they been rejected? Were they being studied?

Over time it became clear to Ernie and his colleagues that the Suggestion System was a sham. Management really didn't want ideas from mere employees. The "system" was a way to "blow off steam" but nothing ever really changed because of suggestions from subordinates. In fact, people with ideas for changes or improvements were often "punished" as troublemakers or weirdos. Thus, the office employees developed a new system of their own for feedback; that is, for "making certain demands."

How might Arthur Higgerty improve the process? First, it is important to really want to know what people think. If a manager is not sincere, it is better not to ask. A formal system that is relegated to the personnel department cannot take the place of a managerial style that encourages feedback and ideas for improvement on a continuing basis. Organizations get better in a thousand little ways. Therefore, it is important to "uncover" as many ideas possible. The law of large numbers applies: The best way to get a good idea is to first have a lot of ideas.

Ideas are fragile. They have to be treated with care—acknowledged and nurtured. It is important not to dampen the enthusiasm of proponents, regardless of the "obvious" merits or demerits of proposals. Ideas that prove useful should be rewarded expeditiously. A positive climate is crucial to offset two basic human barriers to creativity—self-censorship and group negativism.

If Ernie thinks that an embryonic notion is "too far out" to be expressed out loud, the organization is deprived of a potentially useful idea. If any ideas that do get expressed are immediately pooh-poohed or dumped on, the organization may be stifling creativity. If people feel "punished" for making suggestions, they will stop making them. Then, the only feedback to management will be complaints (rather than positive suggestions) in the form of petitions or anonymous letters or the paper-bag approach that Ernie and his group have adopted.

Some organizations, like 3M, have tried to develop a positive climate with a constant reminder: "Don't be caught stifling a potentially good idea." This means that constructive dissatisfaction is not only allowed, it is encouraged and rewarded. This is not easy. It is uncomfortable. Vested interests are often threatened. But individual and organizational well-being can benefit from an ingrained process of introspection and renewal. It is too easy to be complacent. One way to offset this natural tendency is to bring as many minds as possible to bear on the problem of improving what we do and how we do it.

Key Points to Remember

1. Most people have the potential to contribute ideas for improvement; many minds can be better than one.

2. Be sincere when soliciting feedback and suggestions; otherwise don't ask. Recognize that participation can make managing more complex and difficult.

3. Make it clear that all ideas are welcome—even those that seem strange or "far out."

4. Acknowledge suggestions as quickly as possible and nurture them carefully, *then* evaluate them thoroughly.

5. Cultivate an overall climate where constructive dissatisfaction is encouraged and rewarded.

EUREKA: CREATIVITY CREATION

Creativity is a word that smacks of goodness. Like efficiency or excellence it becomes a platitude. Of course we all want it. The question is: How do we get it? How can we manage it? The idea of managing creativity may seem like a paradox—the meanings of these two words seem incongruent. Creativity is thought of as something free and unfettered while management connotes regulation and control. However, if we examine the conditions under which creativity occurs we can see ways in which we can encourage and facilitate creative thinking.

The cartoon suggests two ideas to pursue. The first is that somehow creativity is related to intelligence. Creativity is usually defined in terms of attributes that lead to novel, useful, and understandable ideas or products. While this attribute is marginally related to intelligence—it is slightly more likely that bright people will be creative—a high IQ doesn't seem to be a major contributor. And for that, most of us should be thankful. By the time people are employed in organizations, their intelligence (as measured by IQ tests) tends to be fairly stable.

The second idea present in the cartoon is that all it would take is a shift in the lab technician's thinking to get the ladder through the door. It is a new way of thinking about objects or concepts—a novel combination of ideas. This is creative thinking.

The issue for managers is how such creative thinking can be encouraged. It is not something that can be produced on demand or induced by the use of deadlines or threats. It is something that needs to be nurtured and developed.

Probably the two most central aspects to creative thinking are divergent thought and freedom. By divergent thought we mean exposure to different ideas and different perspectives on the same problem. The research on creativity has shown over and over again that having novel ideas is related to new ways of thinking about or looking at things.

In the organizational context, think tanks, ''skunk works,'' brainstorming groups, and quality circles often bring people together to simply generate ideas. Techniques such as delphi or nominal groups have also proven useful in facilitating creative thinking. These various approaches have a number of aspects in common. First, they bring people together from different areas or jobs, or levels. Second, they encourage idea generation WITHOUT CRITICISM during the initial stages. Evaluation of ideas occurs later and usually without directly tying an idea to a particular person. Thus, the fear of social ridicule is greatly reduced.

This latter idea emphasizes freedom as well. People need to feel both free and encouraged to tell others about their ideas. The delphi and nominal group techniques are specifically designed to reduce the fear and apprehension of being ridiculed for one's novel ideas.

Other things can be done. Like everything else, if you truly want to stimulate creativity you need to let people have *time* to do it and to *reward* it. Thinking takes time and even though it might not look like people are working when they are sitting at their desks staring out the window, they may be doing their most important work. And you have to encourage people to fail. Not all new ideas are good ones. In fact, most probably are not. But even if one in ten is good, it is usually well worth the effort. So, give it time, encourage it, develop it, and recognize it.

The result is usually more good ideas. But additional benefits are that people feel freer and more enthusiastic about their work. Creativity creation often leads to more satisfaction and a spirit of innovation. And happy employees as well as innovative ones will go a long way to make the organization more effective.

Key Points to Remember

1. Creativity leads to novel, useful, and understandable ideas.

2. The creative process can be managed; that is, the conditions can be provided to encourage and develop and reward creative thought.

3. People need to feel safe to bring up new ideas. They need to feel like they will not be ridiculed and that their ideas will be seriously considered.

4. Employees need time to be creative and they need to be rewarded for trying (and failing) as well as for succeeding.

A BOOK AND ITS COVER: DISCRIMINATION

People in organizations today come in all shapes, sizes, and colors: Young and old, male and female, black and yellow and white. We're all different. However, most of the power, money, influence, and top positions are held by white males. And for a long time women and nonwhite males have been held back in terms of education, salaries, power, and almost every other attribute in our society that reflects status.

This cartoon points out an all too common phenomenon: women are not taken seriously. They are treated as if their sexual attractiveness is related to their effectiveness. Well, as we all know, the legal climate has changed dramatically over the last 25 years and while blatant comments like the one in the cartoon are less likely now, there are still numerous examples of sexism or racism that occur.

Most of the major issues such as hiring, firing, appraising, and promoting are partially protected by the law. Making these decisions based on race, gender, religion, or age is illegal and wrong. There is no evidence that shows that minorities, women, or older people are unable to perform effectively at almost all jobs (some exceptions have been made for certain jobs requiring very specific skills). What the evidence does show is that on almost any personal attribute dimension (empathy, assertiveness) or cognitive capability (intelligence, analytical thinking) or physical attribute (strength, dexterity) there is a normal distribution of the characteristic in the population at large and in subpopulations.

Nonetheless, subtle forms of discrimination still take place. One of the most obvious indications is the language that is used. Good guys wear white hats; managers are male; and secretaries are female. These sorts of assumptions show up in our language all the time in terms of the pronouns we use and the symbolism represented in the message. There has been a concerted effort to make our language gender and race neutral, but we have a long way to go. Look at job descriptions, formal documents, and organization manuals and see what sort of language is used. Change them if they need it.

A second form of subtle discrimination takes the form of stereotypes or expectations. Why should we assume that older people don't want taxing tasks; that women should make the coffee; or that blacks are athletic or musical? Don't assume that others are not aware of the underlying beliefs that prompt such expectations. And don't believe it doesn't bother them. It does.

The obvious point, again, is that each individual is unique, with his or her own set of strengths and weaknesses. The critical issue is to evaluate people based on *relevant criteria* and to match strengths with appropriate tasks. By being blind to color, gender, religion, and age you can utilize people to their maximum potential. Such actions are not only legal, they are effective and are ethically the correct thing to do.

Key Points to Remember

1. It is illegal to discriminate based on race, religion, gender, or age.

2. Subtle clues in language and expectations will give away underlying attitudes that are inappropriate.

3. People know when you hold racist or sexist feelings. It shows up in various ways and they don't like it.

4. Each person has a unique set of skills and being sensitive to his or her race, religion, gender, and age is the right thing to do.

V

Being a Manager

I MUST BE IN MIDDLE MANAGEMENT... I ALWAYS FEEL LIKE I'M BETWEEN A ROCK AND A HARD PLACE.

BEING A MANAGER

Strange as it may seem, Frank and Ernest have survived long enough to become managers. They now belong to a select group of people who perform managerial functions—coordinating human, material, and financial resources to accomplish objectives. Familiar examples are the foreman on an assembly line, the charge nurse, the head librarian, the vice principal, the lead engineer, the chief accountant, and the captain of a spacecraft. ''Manager'' is often used synonymously with other terms such as executive, administrator, supervisor, and boss. Regardless of the specific term or the particular context, the basic functions of a manager remain the same. On the other hand, it is important to ''know the territory'' so that managerial behavior can be tailored to the situation. Managing a restaurant emphasizes different skills than managing a computer assembly line. A fundamental aspect of managing is captured by Frank when he describes middle management as being between a rock and hard place.

Dilemmas abound in the managerial role. New first-line supervisors are often ''caught'' between their former co-workers and middle management. Bosses are often called on to referee squabbles between subordinates. Middle managers, in translating strategies into operational tactics, often have to temper vision with reality. General managers have to resolve conflicts between accounting and marketing or design and manufacturing. Top executives are involved in balancing the interests of all stakeholders—customers, suppliers, owners, employees, and the public. The complexity at this level goes beyond the concept of between. The strategy formulation and implementation process can often create a feeling of being ''*among* many rocks and hard places.''

Organizations become effective and efficient by doing the right things, in the right way, at the right time, and with a high ratio of output to input. Achieving excellent performance—and ensuring the continuing capability to perform—is the job of management. It means getting quality work done on time. Management is work—just as doctoring, selling, building, and teaching, are work. However, it is not the individual performance of a task. The essence of management is coordination of people/activities/functions in organizational contexts. It is necessary in a two-person partnership as well as General Motors. Management is mental (thinking, intuiting, feeling) work performed by people at various levels—top, middle, and first-line—in all types of organizations. It is obvious in businesses, schools, hospitals, and government agencies. But it is also necessary for churches, prisons, social clubs, bridge tournaments, climbing expeditions, and an almost infinite variety of group endeavors.

In this section we will illustrate some of the problems and opportunities of being a manager by considering the following topics:

- Assumptions and Stereotypes: Self-fulfilling Prophecies
- If You Want a Job Done Right: Delegating
- Good Intentions: Planning and Implementing
- Where Am I?: Organizing
- Staying on Track: Controlling
- Graphic Feedback: Performance Appraisal

ASSUMPTIONS AND STEREOTYPES: SELF-FULFILLING PROPHECIES

Basic beliefs about people affect our approach to designing work organizations and managing them. Assumptions about basic human nature range from good, industrious, responsible, and smart...to evil, lazy, irresponsible, and dumb. These polar views are unrealistic; people are neither completely good nor completely bad. But we all tend to simplify and categorize other people because it is easier than considering each case on its merits. The way we treat people will be affected by our tendencies to be relatively positive/optimistic or relatively negative/pessimistic. In this episode the manager appears to have a rather negative and pessimistic view of Frank's capabilities. He is "behind the eight ball" and would be starting a job with "two strikes against him." He might succeed, but the probabilities are not good.

The basic assumptions a manager makes can have a significant effect on individuals and organizations. Personal interactions evolve in certain ways: compensation systems are designed, communication patterns are developed, authority-responsibility relationships are identified, planning/control processes are established, and many other pertinent organizational characteristics are affected by managers' assumptions about the nature and capabilities of the people involved. For example, negative assumptions can lead to tight control, little delegation, constant checking, and a stifling and demoralizing atmosphere.

The concept of self-fulfilling prophecies—the Pygmalion effect—is particularly important for managers. It suggests that the expectation of something can actually cause it to happen. And it works both ways. If we assume the worst, something bad will happen. If we assume the best, something good will happen. Positive assumptions lead to challenging assignments, encouraging feedback, coaching. The likelihood of good performance increases. On the other hand, if a manager thinks that Frank is incompetent, he will not be given much opportunity to perform. Thus, he will not have the experience necessary for promotion. Eventually he will quit or be fired. Given the power of self-fulfilling prophecies, negative stereotypes—minorities, women, oldtimers, youngsters, whomever—can have devastating effects.

The Pygmalion effect is more than the power of positive thinking. It is not magic; there are some key ingredients. It is important for managers to reflect as much optimism as possible until they are convinced otherwise. The phrase "as much as possible" allows situational analysis and a realistic approach that recognizes differences in goodness, industriousness, intelligence, and reliability. Within an accepting, encouraging climate, positive Pygmalions create high performance expectations—challenging, realistic goals that are accepted—for their subordinates. And they facilitate achievement and satisfaction by providing lots of feedback about performance, including praise and correction focused on specific incidents. They are confident about their ability for developing people and therefore work hard to make their prophecy come true. Organizations that are managed on such a positive note tend to be more satisfying for participants and they can be more effective and efficient as well.

Key Points to Remember

1. Managers' expectations—either positive or negative—can increase the probability that something good or bad will happen.

2. Pessimistic assumptions, even if they are accurate for a few people, can lead to stifling overcontrol and serious negative effects for the organization as a whole.

3. Optimistic assumptions can lead to a positive climate that includes accepting and encouraging people, giving them opportunities to perform, and providing lots of feedback.

4. High performance expectations—challenging, realistic goals that are accepted—are the foundation of the Pygmalion effect.

5. Prophecies are fulfilled when managers help subordinates achieve their goals by providing the necessary means, relevant training, and coaching when appropriate.

IF YOU WANT A JOB DONE RIGHT: DELEGATING

"If you want a job done right, do it yourself." This old adage can seriously damage managerial effectiveness. Managers are paid for coordinating the work of others, not doing it. But the maxim is seductive, particularly for perfectionists. When things are not done exactly the way they would like, they are tempted to take over and do them "right." And because it works, they feel rewarded and are likely to keep on doing it.

The other side of the coin can also be dangerous; that is, dumping everything on someone else. Some managers, like our friend in this episode, assume they can relax in their new role and delegate everything. In a sense, they continue to "pass the buck" downward as well as upward and sideways. They don't understand the true meaning of delegation—giving up authority and retaining responsibility. Poor Ernie is in for a rough time with his new boss. He is likely to get the tough assignments as well as all the dirty jobs and insignificant tasks.

A pessimistic view of others' capabilities restrains managers from delegating tasks to them. The negative consequences abound. We stifle potential motivation by not allowing people to do what they are trained to do. We constrain the growth and development of subordinates. And we also strain the mental and physical limits of managers.

How can delegation work for the benefit of individuals and organizations? A basic element is recognizing the need to empower people to contribute. A positive view of subordinates' capabilities is also important. If there is a lack of knowledge or skill, a manager needs to be optimistic about the chances for them to learn and develop through experience. Employees should be allowed to learn from mistakes, as long as they are not too costly. Another important aspect is tolerance for different ways of doing things. It is easy to delegate to clones—those subordinates who are molded in the boss's image. In such a case the boss can be sure that things will be done his/her way without much direction. Another bit of insurance is a very strong culture that is internalized by all organization members. A well-understood set of values, beliefs, and attitudes provides norms for the way things are to be done. Delegating becomes easier in such cases.

Effective delegation requires clear expectations so that there are no surprises. If only results count, then there should be no second guessing about means. If there is concern about methods as well as results, then it should be made clear at the outset. Delegation works best if a manager gives up the authority necessary for accomplishing the task and retains the ultimate responsibility for the subordinate's work. This is a subtle but powerful point that needs to be emphasized.

When a task is delegated, the boss needs to "keep in touch" so that questions can be answered or problems can be solved. But it is not a good idea to "hover"...just in case. This kind of behavior can undermine the confidence of a subordinate and negate the initial positive vibes.

Effective managers maintain a contingency view, i.e., they delegate to different degrees depending on the capabilities and willingness of subordinates. Also, an important assignment can be rewarding for some people but not for everyone. In general, however, delegation is a means for managers to extend their influence, bring as many resources as possible to bear on the task, and emphasize their role in coordinating the work of others.

Key Points to Remember

1. Resist the temptation to believe that doing it yourself is the only way to "get it right."

2. Don't "dump" everything on others just because it is a managerial prerogative.

3. Develop a strong culture with relevant norms for behavior. Then set forth clear expectations for results (and methods if need be).

4. Managers are responsible for the growth and development of their subordinates. Allow people to make mistakes and learn from experience.

5. Provide the authority necessary to get a delegated task done.

6. Differentiate the degree of delegation according to the individual and the situation.

GOOD INTENTIONS: PLANNING AND IMPLEMENTING

"The road to hell is paved with good intentions" is an adage that describes New Year's resolutions and organizational strategies. A list of resolutions or a multi-colored planning document can be very impressive. But they are hollow exercises unless something happens, i.e., they are implemented effectively and enthusiastically. Our friend in this cartoon is a prime example of what can go wrong. Planning becomes an exercise that is not taken seriously by the people who must implement the results.

Goal setting and planning are means of defining intentions—deciding in advance what is to be done and how. In organizations it involves determining overall missions, identifying areas in which key results are sought, and setting specific objectives. It also involves developing policies, programs, and procedures for achieving the desired outcomes. Planning provides a framework for integrating the decisions made in various subunits, at different levels in the organization, and at different times. Plans or intentions are always based on premises about the future. Whether consciously or unconsciously, managers consider environmental opportunities in terms of factors such as politics, economics, demographics, technology, and competition. They analyze the strengths and weaknesses of the organization as they relate to the opportunities. Because personal desires are often stirred into the planning process it is not always easy to develop an objective description of past performance, current conditions, and future trends.

The basic elements of planning—long look ahead, broad look around, and a searching look within—are straightforward. The process of developing a comprehensive strategy should be kept as simple as possible. And it should be considered a *process*, not an event. This is where individuals and organizations often fall off the trail. They engage in sophisticated "exercises" to develop elaborate plans that look good and read well— but are never implemented. What can be done?

One approach is to avoid paralysis by analysis—the tendency to gather a little more information, to rework the data, to check with a few more people, or to uncover another reason for caution. Of course, precipitous, capricious action is not recommended for long-run success. However, errors of omission can be as serious as errors of commission. Perfectionism that leads to procrastination has to be replaced by activism on the part of individuals and organizations. A moderately good plan that is implemented enthusiastically is more effective than a perfect plan that doesn't "get off the ground."

In general, the amount of effort involved in implementation is a function of the manager's ability to influence others--subordinates, peers, and bosses. Assuming adequate financial, technological, and material resources, performance depends on the degree to which latent human capability is tapped. The key factors are leadership skills and motivated participants. Long-run commitment is fostered by a clear vision and a strong culture. Charisma can help build excitement and enthusiasm, but the key factor is a meaningful strategy—goals and plans that make sense to those who must implement them.

Another important approach to improving the implementation of plans is to involve as many doers as possible in the process. People "in the trenches" may be able to contribute substantive suggestions during the planning process. They may have information, perspectives, and ideas that can improve the final product. They can provide a reality check that tests feasibility. Involvement in planning is an educational process that increases the probability that people will know both the *why* of plans and *how* to carry them out. Involvement increases "ownership" and commitment— important ingredients in generating, directing, and sustaining the effort needed to accomplish goals. Delegation, self-management, and autonomous work teams are a means of enriching the work by adding planning to doing. These managerial approaches challenge the traditional separation of work; namely, that managers plan and workers implement the plans. The modern view emphasizes a joint endeavor that empowers people to use their talents effectively and efficiently.

Key Points to Remember

1. Plans, like goals, are intentions that are meaningless without the actions necessary to implement them.

2. Comprehensive, long-range strategies must be translated into operational tactics in order to be useful in guiding behavior.

3. Planning is not an event that takes place periodically and then is forgotten while the organization "gets back to work." It is an ongoing process that evolves continually based on performance and feedback.

4. Explicit attention to planning does not ensure success, but it does increase the probability that opportunities will be seized and that potential pitfalls will be avoided.

5. Involvement in the planning process improves the probability that implementors will be knowledgeable and committed. This can lead to the enthusiastic effort that is needed to get from intentions to results.

WHERE AM I?: ORGANIZING

Once upon a time organizations had stable, simple, straightforward structures that gave everyone involved a good idea of "where they stood." The organization chart clearly depicted the chain of command, i.e., authority-responsibility relationships. Each person had only one boss and each boss was supposed to have a relatively standard span of control. Communications were designed to flow up and down and across the chart. To report or inquire otherwise meant one was "out of line." Then a funny thing happened on the way to the future. The world in general and the world of work in particular got more complex. And as Frank and Ernie have discovered, the straightforward organization chart became a jumbled maze.

Organization structures and processes should flow from strategy. Managers are responsible for developing and maintaining structures and processes for carrying out plans and achieving relevant goals. Developing a structure involves dividing the work into meaningful components and then integrating the results. Patterns of relationships are often defined by organization charts and work-flow diagrams. A chart typically shows the divisions of work, line or staff roles, and vertical relationships that indicate authority, responsibility, and accountability. Flow diagrams depict the transformation process used in producing goods or services.

The dilemma that Frank and Ernie find themselves in is common today. The environment of work organizations has become increasingly turbulent. There is an accelerating change of pace in technology. Population keeps increasing relentlessly. People are more mobile than ever before. The economy is more volatile. Industry demarcations are becoming blurred. Political systems are less stable. The values, beliefs, and attitudes of employees, at all levels, are not what they used to be. Everything seems more temporary and dynamic.

In response, organization structures and processes have been adapted over the years. First came *upsizing* to take advantage of economies of scale. Then came *capsizing* because organizations became too large, unwieldy, and often top heavy. Big is not bad per se, but the ineffectiveness, inefficiency, unresponsiveness, slack resources, and low morale that often accompany bigness hamper performance. The rage in the 1980s was *downsizing*, based on the idea that small is beautiful. In most cases this meant fewer layers in the hierarchy in order to facilitate communication and speed up decision making. In some cases it meant smaller autonomous units in order to pinpoint accountability. There have been suggestions for *upsidedowning*—revising the typical pyramid organization structure in order to emphasize management's role in "supporting" the operators who do the real work in the organization. The visual effect of this concept lends credence to the idea of streamlining and eliminating the dead weight that often "rests" on the shelves of the pyramid. The current plea is for *rightsizing*—a contingency view that emphasizes the need to "fit" the organization structure (size, shape, fluidity, etc.) to the situation.

Organizations can become too large or too tall or too wide or too loose or too tight. When the official organization structure and processes no longer seem functional, its members often develop informal ways of relating and getting the work done. Indeed, one way to stifle productivity is to follow established (obsolete?) procedures and lines of authority. It follows then, that a promising approach to organization design is to analyze the existing system and see what actually works—not what is supposed to happen. We typically find personal power that goes beyond positional authority. We find alignments and allegiances that develop because of the energy, expertise, and wisdom of certain people. We find adjustments and accommodations that are not covered in job descriptions and procedures manuals. The danger, of course, is that by formalizing the informal, we will "kill" the spirit reflected in current efforts to operate effectively and efficiently.

Finding and implementing the appropriate organization design is not easy. Drawing or redrawing organization charts and flow diagrams is not the essence of organizing. Improvement implies change and the ultimate test is behavior. True flexibility is the willingness of operators and managers to implement the behavior that is necessary to make any structure or process work.

Key Points to Remember

1. There is no one best way to organize; a contingency approach is called for in order to fit the design to the situation.

2. Organization structures and processes should flow from strategy; they are part of the means for achieving goals.

3. An accelerating change of pace along many dimensions suggests the need for flexibility—the ability to adapt to circumstances as they arise.

4. Study the informal organization—dotted lines, diagonal relationships, ad hoc groups, etc.—to learn how the work actually gets down. Gently incorporate the best features into new designs without stifling spontaneity and creativity.

5. The ultimate test of organizing or reorganizing is effective and efficient behavior. Charts and flow diagrams are the tip of the iceberg.

STAYING ON TRACK: CONTROLLING

Being "in control" is obviously better than being "out of control." But what does control mean in an organizational context? To some it means curbing or restraining; to others it means steering or guiding. A more important question, perhaps, is: What should be curbed or restrained or steered or guided? The CIA scenario shows a focus on hours worked, but in reality the factor being controlled may be hours "at work" rather than "hours worked." There can be a significant difference.

Eight of the ten commandments (Exodus 20:1-26) are negative or restraining; only two are positive guidelines for behavior. Much of our behavior is shaped by negative controls—lists or manuals about what not to do. We like to think of control in the more positive sense because it is essential in organizational life. Coordination, the essence of management, requires control—maintaining organizational activity within allowable limits, as measured from expectations set forth in goals and plans.

Good managers concentrate on monitoring relevant characteristics. They focus on key goals and action plans even if they are difficult to measure and evaluate. It is tempting to focus on dimensions that are easily quantified and measurable, regardless of how relevant they are. This is dangerous because organizations "get what they measure" in terms of the behavior of participants. Paying attention to irrelevant criteria gives the wrong signal about what is important.

Managing includes concern for both *what* is accomplished (output/results) and *how* things are done (legal means/efficient use of resources/morale of participants). When outcomes are difficult to measure it is necessary to focus more on behavior, on the assumption that appropriate behavior will lead to good organizational performance. The means used to control any process can be highly programmed, mechanistic, and computerized. But when the issue is controlling behavior, subjective impressions are involved. Human judgment is required to establish standards and decide when behavior is "inappropriate."

Indirect controls can play a large role in maintaining behavior within allowable limits. Strong organizational cultures lead to homogeneous value systems, internalization of group norms, and the acceptance of guidelines and limits. Direct controls also play a major role in both restraining and guiding behavior. Laws, regulations, policies, and procedures are all means of controlling the behavior of individuals and organizations. The EPA, OSHA, NLRB, EEOC, et al., provide long lists of prescriptions and proscriptions that control organizational behavior. Policy and procedures manuals often do the same thing. The ''flavor'' is predominantly negative, with attention focused on what can't be done.

Control processes can be specific and tight when need be or when circumstances allow. Quality is often a function of precision manufacturing to close tolerances. On the other hand, maintaining customer goodwill at a desired level is not as straightforward. We often have to be satisfied with gross indicators of effectiveness—how things ''feel.'' Regardless of the ease or difficulty of measuring performance, the process is the same. Goals and plans must be evident and understood. Otherwise, there is nothing to control against. There must be some means of measuring results, progress, or conditions. . . ranging from electronic gauges to gut feelings. And there must be some means of adjusting the processes in order to get back ''on target.'' Renewed or redirected effort may be required. Or new materials. Or new equipment. Some sort of change must be possible or else the control process is meaningless and management is frustrated.

Tommy Lasorda, manager of the Los Angeles Dodgers, once described good managing as like holding a dove in your hand. ''Squeeze it too tight and you kill it. Hold it too loose and it flies away.'' This is the essence of good controlling—enough but not too much. With human behavior, overcontrol can be devastating in terms of both immediate and long-run effects. On the other hand, a laissez faire approach can be equally detrimental. Without the restraining, correcting, and guiding that is part of the control process, there is no learning and no improvement. So controlling really is an art—enough attention to keep individual or organizational endeavor within allowable limits, enough correction to facilitate learning, but not so much that effort and improvement are stifled.

Key Points to Remember

1. Controlling is intertwined with and dependent on goals and plans.

2. The positive connotation of control—guiding—has a better psychological effect on people than the negative connotation—curbing or restraining.

3. Concentrate on monitoring relevant criteria—key goals, important plans, and behavior that is necessary for success.

4. Use indirect control—organization culture, group norms, and personal integrity—whenever feasible. Rely on self-control as much as possible.

5. Use direct control—budget reviews, performance appraisals, and quality inspection—as gently as possible in order that correction and guidance can occur with causing dysfunctional resentment.

GRAPHIC FEEDBACK: PERFORMANCE APPRAISAL

So you want to know how you're doing. Seems like a simple request, yet many employees cite lack of feedback as a major problem. But maybe no news is good news. Or, as Frank once said to Ernie: "The only time the boss ever notices what I do is when I don't do it." Sometimes the message is unclear, like: "Not half bad, Smythe." In the example below we assume the boss is trying to clearly emphasize Edgarton's shortcomings with visual aids and the pejorative moniker "pinhead."

What is the first thing that comes to mind when you are asked to respond to the word *evaluate*? Typical responses are criticism, apprehension, rating, and failure. Such feelings are the result of actual experience and yet the real meaning of evaluate is "to find value in." Why the overwhelming negative connotation of a seemingly positive and natural process? In many cases performance appraisal has become an elaborate system for rating people or judging merit and then using the results to determine compensation. Somehow the use of feedback for praising good performance and for changing goals or behavior has gotten lost in a shuffle of paper work.

A lot of time, effort, and money has been spent on designing the perfect appraisal form for evaluating traits and behaviors. Some are better than others, but no form—filled out and filed—can substitute for a face-to-face discussion about expectations and results. And it is the appraisal discussion that is usually missing. Horror stories abound. "My boss and I haven't talked about my performance since I finished six months probation three years ago." Understandably, discussions with "problem" subordinates are often avoided. But even potentially positive discussions are also avoided. One assistant manager reported: "I asked my boss for some feedback this year and he said he didn't want to talk about it. Fearing that I was about to be fired, I went to Personnel to see how he had rated me. Surprise! The evaluation was glowing and I was scheduled for an above average raise, but we didn't talk about it."

The primary purpose of performance appraisal is to compare actual results with desired results and to design action plans that will close any gaps. The essence is guidance, coaching, and development for continuing improvement. The focus is typically individual, but it could be a team or department as well. The evaluation process is critical for progress; individuals and units must know "how they're doing" in order to focus time and energy appropriately. Praise can keep things going in the right direction. Criticism is ineffective unless it is accompanied by goal setting and action planning that is initiated by, or at least accepted by, the subordinate.

Several key decisions have to be made about performance appraisal systems. One is to separate review and planning discussions from compensation decisions. The spectre of money creates tension and stifles candid evaluations. Compensation usually depends on more than current performance. It gets confounded by length of service, comparative worth, equity, and other special circumstances. Second, it should be an integral part of day-to-day managing; *not* a series of separate events—particularly *annual* reviews. Third, the process should be as positive as possible. This means recognizing specific accomplishments as well as improvements in behavior. It does not mean ignoring problems or needed corrective action. Another crucial element, which many bosses consistently neglect, is to let the subordinate speak first about *both* "things done well" *and* "things to do better." This gives the evaluator a chance to reinforce the positive and concur with suggestions for improvement. And it encourages people to be accountable to themselves as well as to the boss and the organization.

Given the current emphasis on teamwork in organizations—project teams, task forces, autonomous work units—the use of peer reviews can be beneficial in improving and individual and group performance. The key is to establish relevant criteria and then to provide timely feedback to people from those who have firsthand knowledge about how things are going. When bosses become part of the team, rather than overseers, they receive feedback as well. Indeed, bosses might benefit from subordinate reviews of their performance in any situation.

Key Points to Remember

1. Evaluate means "to find value in." It takes conscious effort because criticism—finding fault—is so natural for human beings. It is important to recognize specific accomplishments and progress, however slight.

2. Appraisal forms, however sophisticated, are not a substitute for review discussions that are the heart of the appraisal process.

3. Review-appraisal-evaluation discussions should be an integral part of managing and improving any endeavor. They allow the manager to be more of a constant coach and less of a periodic critic.

4. By engaging in self-appraisal, subordinates become more accountable, their ideas and energy are tapped, and problem solving becomes a joint process that focuses on goal setting and action planning.

5. Peer evaluations for team members can be helpful in improving individual and group performance.

PART

VI

Being a Leader

BEING A LEADER

What is leadership? Is it some mysterious quality with which a few lucky individuals are imbued? Are we born with it, do we learn it, or does the situation make the leader? These questions have concerned management for a long time.

As we see from the cartoon on page 73, Frank and Ernie have a boss who says "no" all the time. Many of us have had similar encounters. However, the picture suggests that the boss is a grumpy sort of fellow and that somehow saying no was an inappropriate response or a poor leadership style. The research results suggest a more qualified approach.

There have been thousands of studies on leadership. The two major questions addressed are who becomes a leader and which leaders are most effective. The first question has floundered, because authors can't agree on whether being a leader implies holding a certain type of job or the possession of certain traits or characteristics. The consensus seems to be the former position—that *leaders* hold positions that involve the direction and coordination of others and that different types of people ascend to these positions.

Leadership, however, implies that the person is a good leader, that he or she is doing something right. And here we have a slightly more focused question: What sort of style differentiates good leaders from the poor ones? Some characteristics seem to help. Bright leaders generally do better than not so bright leaders. Having energy, enthusiasm, and interpersonal skills seems to help as well. But even after exhaustive studies we can't do much better than flipping a coin to predict performance.

What seems to be far more important is a match between leadership style and a *particular* setting. Studies conducted by different researchers at different institutions actually seemed to agree in their descriptions of leadership style. The basic two dimensions that emerge refer to one's emphasis on the *task* and on one's emphasis on *interpersonal relations*. A leader can be high or low on one or both dimensions. The critical issue is the match between the style and the demands of the situation.

Researchers learned how to describe settings. Work in this area has produced some consistent findings. Interpersonal skills help when there are lots of different types of people involved and group interaction is important. Task skills help when structuring and direction are needed. So factors such as the amount of structure in the task, the interaction required, and the power of the leader seem to make a difference in terms of what style works best.

The evidence suggests that every style has its place and no one style is best. In some cases leaders need to adjust their style to fit the setting and in others they must change the setting to fit their style. A number of leadership training programs emphasize diagnostic skills. Leaders who are trained to diagnose their style and the situation and adjust tend to do better than those who are less aware and less flexible.

We will develop these ideas further via the following topics:

- I'm Right Behind You: Followership
- Trickle Up: Participative Decision Making
- The Ins and Outs: Membership
- The Terminator: Firing
- Sit Right Down: Open Door Policy

RIGHT BEHIND YOU: FOLLOWERSHIP

Most leaders are also followers, i.e., they have bosses. Thus, they need to manage up as well as down. Subordinates often go to extremes such as fawning obedience or militant insubordination. When a manager is new, some subordinates seize the opportunity to ''set the boss straight'' on how things are done around here. They want to let the ''new person on the block'' know about the existing culture. Frank seems to be a graduate of obedience training. He let his manager know, ''in no uncertain terms,'' who the boss is. However, Frank's statement implies an aggressive approach that disintegrated into confirmation that the new manager would, in fact, be the boss.

Managing the boss effectively requires maintaining a functional working relationship. Uncritical dependence is not functional in the long run; nor is passivity or insubordination. One should attempt to understand the boss's perspective—the context of the job, the priorities among goals, and attitudes concerning appropriate behavior at work. Observing the boss's behavior provides clues to attitudes about what is important, correct, and probably expected of others. In general, one should help the boss be effective and feel competent as a manager.

Leading and following is an interactive process that results in reciprocal influence. For example, the more subordinates exhibit competence and self-control, the more the leader can delegate authority. The more the leader hovers and second guesses, the more subordinates are likely to become dependent or alienated. Effective following does not call for sheeplike behavior. On the contrary, the best approach is to strive to achieve obvious organizational goals through teamwork as well as independent critical thinking and action when necessary. This may backfire with a boss that favors personal loyalty and obedience over organizational commitment and performance. However, in such cases, it may be wise to clear out your desk and move on.

Followership includes recognition that most bosses are human and therefore need and desire feedback. Provide constructive criticism *when asked*. Include authentic feedback concerning the positive and negative impact of the boss's behavior. Praise the boss when things are done well. Positive reinforcement from followers can help shape the behavior of leaders in ways that are mutually beneficial. This is particularly important in areas that are crucial for organizational success and for maintaining healthy working conditions and high morale.

Like Frank, most of the time subordinates can adapt to a boss's style in order to develop a smooth working relationship. Slight adjustments to one's natural approach can be made relatively easily. Different styles can be advantageous if they are complementary. But extreme differences may be difficult to cope with. If the boss's expectations are counter to one's own values and ethical standards (or one's understanding of what the organization expects) the subordinate has a dilemma. He or she can confront the issue and "let the chips fall where they may" or adapt to the situation. The first alternative is risky; the second alternative may result in lingering resentment that affects future relations and performance. There is a fine line between assertiveness and aggressiveness. The former may be seen as concerned involvement; the latter may be seen as disloyal insubordination.

Key Points to Remember

1. Effective followership is an important managerial skill and can be a training ground for leadership.

2. Take time to understand the boss's perspective on relevant issues—goals, priorities, values, beliefs, and attitudes.

3. Make sure what's expected of you; don't assume too much or take things for granted.

4. Make the boss look good and feel as competent as possible without sacrificing your own integrity.

5. Be a committed team player; provide honest opinions when asked; and exhibit independent critical thinking when appropriate.

TRICKLE UP: PARTICIPATION DECISION MAKING

Leaders are constantly required to make decisions, some of them tough decisions that have substantial impact on people or the profitability of the company. The question that often confronts a leader is: "Should I get input from others?"

The cartoon depicts just this sort of situation—a leader asking a subordinate for an opinion. However, it also suggests that this request for input is insincere and a sham. All the leader wants is an affirmation that he is correct.

The problem, of course, is that all too often participation takes this form. In fact, one of our other units, "The Suggestion System," deals with just this issue: information solicited through a participation process must be taken seriously and used when applicable. Otherwise, people will soon realize they are being manipulated and refuse to participate.

Participation has a "political" side. It makes people feel important to be asked for their opinion. It helps them to understand what decisions are being made and why. It clarifies issues for them. It gives them some sense of control. These can be important benefits of participation. "What do you think?" is a heavy tonic for self-esteem.

But a second, and equally important, issue is whether participation in decision making works. Does having a subordinate participate in the decision-making process make the decision better? The results here are far less clear.

The most comprehensive review of this literature, conducted by Ed Locke, suggested that participation does not necessarily result in better decisions. About a third of the studies show a positive effect, a third show no effect, and a third show a negative effect. On the other hand, a majority of the studies show a positive effect on job satisfaction. So, participation, in general (i.e., across different settings) does lead to higher satisfaction but may not lead to greater effectiveness.

When faced with these results a number of people tried to determine when participation seemed to work. Vic Vroom and Phil Yetton developed a comprehensive diagnostic model and training program to help leaders choose the type and amount of participation that is needed for particular decisions. This contingency approach is one of the best models we have in this area.

First, managers are required to ask a series of questions about the decision context. For example, they need to ask (1) Is there any way that we can really determine if this is a good or bad decision? (2) Do I have all the information I need? (3) Do subordinates have information I need? (4) Can I trust subordinates to give me accurate information? (5) Will subordinates carry out the decision without participation? The set of combinations or patterns of responses to these questions produce a typology of situations. Then for each situation the appropriate level of participation is selected.

The degree of participation should vary. On one extreme the leader makes the decision while at the other extreme there could be a group discussion with consensus or majority rule. When a leader has all the information that is needed and she is confident that subordinates will implement her decision, participation is unnecessary. Where subordinates have important information and need to be included in order to ensure implementation, then participation is obviously appropriate.

This model has been developed using thousands of managers dealing with real decisions. The training has been used for years and demonstrated to be effective. The overwhelming consensus is that different types of decisions require different degrees of participation and leaders have to diagnose each situation and select the correct level for effective decision making.

Finally, at an organizational level it is clear that participation is receiving significant attention and having an impact. Quality circles, autonomous work teams, job enrichment and job ownership all emphasize the need for individual and group input. Management is recognizing that there can be a ''trickle up'' as well as a ''trickle down'' process.

Key Points to Remember

1. Participation is both a political and a social issue. People feel important and part of the system if they participate.

2. Participation as a general style for all decisions does not increase effectiveness, but it does increase job satisfaction.

3. Leaders need to diagnose decision situations in terms of what sort of information is needed and the effects of participation on implementation.

4. The proper match of the degree of participation with the particular decision context can increase decision effectiveness and overall satisfaction.

THE INS AND OUTS: MEMBERSHIP

Leaders have expectations about the ways they want their subordinates to behave. These expectations may cover lots of different issues from a dress code to when and how they wish to be talked to. Some people want a formal relationship with plenty of distance while others want closer interpersonal ties. Meeting target dates and being punctual may be critical for certain leaders but less so for others.

THE BOSS FINALLY BROUGHT ME INTO THE DECISION-MAKING PROCESS — HE SAID I COULD SHAPE UP OR SHIP OUT.

THAVES 3-26

The point raised by the cartoon is that these expectations need to be met—at least to some extent—or the person's job is in danger. By "shape up" Frank probably means that he is violating some important expectation held by his boss and that if he doesn't change his ways he is "outta here."

We have already mentioned the fact that different leaders have different styles and that the proper match between style and context is needed for personal and group effectiveness. Well, part of that context includes the characteristics of subordinates: their work habits, values, and personalities. Recognizing this fact is important. It suggests that leaders need to notice the individual differences of their subordinates in order to motivate them, to evaluate them and to give them feedback. Everyone has strengths and weaknesses and personality quirks. It is what makes us unique. However, from a leadership perspective these differences and quirks can present some problems. For example, this information suggests that leaders need to have different styles for different subordinates as well as for different tasks. Again, recognizing this fact limits the generalizations we can make about any particular leadership style.

The research on the topic is interesting. A whole theory of leadership has been developed around these "dyadic links." Some of the major points have considerable importance for understanding leadership. First, as we would expect, there are major differences in the extent to which a subordinate fits or doesn't fit with the leader. Those that are seen favorably by the leader are part of the ingroup while those who are in disfavor are the outgroup. People usually know which one they belong to. The ingroup tends to be more satisfied with their jobs than the outgroup. The ingroup tends to be evaluated more positively and receive favorable treatment such as challenging assignments, or trips, or time off when they want it. The reverse is true for the outgroup. They tend to be disgruntled and they know their standing with the boss.

Another interesting fact is that leader-subordinate linkages or patterns of interaction form fairly quickly. Some research suggests that in just a matter of weeks *both* the leader and subordinate know where they stand. People who end up in the outgroup clearly don't like it. The question is, what are the implications of such status.

Probably the most difficult problem here is the idea that leaders need to treat people differently to maximize motivation and performance yet they have to be very careful not to be unfair. Differential treatment based simply on liking may lead to lower motivation, performance problems, and potential litigation. This tension between wanting to treat people differently and needing to be fair and unprejudicial is a real dilemma because there is no easy solution. The best thing to keep in mind is that any action that may have formal evaluative consequences for a subordinate should be based on relevant motivational and performance criteria rather than simply liking or disliking.

This issue will be of increasing importance with our workforce becoming more heterogeneous. While a manager has to understand the uniqueness of the individual they also have to treat them fairly. Balancing these two demands requires sensitivity as well as fairness.

Key Points to Remember

1. Leaders have fairly clear expectations about subordinate behavior and performance.

2. Leaders usually have a group of people they like and some they like less well.

3. This ingroup-outgroup distinction is known and recognized by the leader and the subordinates.

4. Leaders have to be careful that they do not let their feelings of liking influence their more formal judgments of and behavior toward their subordinates.

THE TERMINATOR: FIRING

Firing employees is a difficult thing for a leader to do under any circumstances. And lately, with many companies facing economic problems, lots of people are being let go for reasons that are independent of their performance. Because of mergers and the combining of jobs and increased responsibilities for particular jobs many people are defined as redundant.

The cartoon depicts a somewhat harsh approach to terminating an employee. The boss seems to even be enjoying it by making a joke out of it. The reality, however, is that most people who have this responsibility get little pleasure out of it. Research on terminating employees has found that almost everyone interviewed says that firing people is one of the most difficult and unpleasant things about their job. Letting people go, especially after lengthy service to the company can be devastating on people's psychological and economic well-being. We've discussed elsewhere the importance of work for individuals. Substantial evidence suggests that when people are unemployed they are physically and psychologically less well than when they are working.

There are really two types of circumstances that lead to someone being fired: for poor performance or because of economic difficulties or structural rearrangements within the company. One situation focuses on the employee as the problem, while the other focuses on the company.

The industrial discipline literature provides us with some insights about the former process: dealing with performance problems. The most frequently given reasons for people being fired are absenteeism, drug abuse, disobedience, disruptive behavior, failure to follow instructions, and inadequate performance. Some of these reasons may obviously overlap. Being absent or on drugs can influence one's output as can poor interpersonal relations. In fact, what tends to happen is that two or three of these problems occur together.

The recommendations are clear and require systematic treatment by the leader. Information needs to be gathered over time about the persons behavior and performance. Multiple incidents over multiple occasions and settings should be documented. The employee should be given a series of progressively punitive responses. Initially there should be a discussion, followed by written warnings, docking of pay, short-term layoff, and termination. The particulars of any plan of discipline are often worked out in a labor contract with a union, but the general principles apply for all employee. Keep good records, keep the employee informed, and treat everyone fairly and with compassion.

The issue of compassion is important. When an organization has to fire someone, either for poor performance or for economic reasons they should try to do it with class and integrity. If an employee admits to psychological problems or chemical dependencies, counseling can be made available and a second chance given. If problems at home are causing absenteeism, perhaps a half-time appointment would work. If the person definitely has to go, then helping them find another job can be a good thing to do (especially if the person is let go for economic reasons). Such counseling and outplacement services are becoming more and more common in large organizations.

These procedures should be used even if someone is laid off for economic reasons. Many middle level managers have had this experience in the last few years. Organizations have commitments to their people just as people have commitments to the organizations. If people have to be fired then everything possible should be done to help them with replacement.

In summary, issues of termination should have the status of an organization *policy*. People who do it and employees who receive it should know what to expect. There is simply no place for the arbitrary and capricious firing of subordinates. It is inappropriate, unfair, personally damaging, potentially inefficient, and, in more and more cases, illegal.

Key Points to Remember

1. Firing is a difficult process for both parties involved. Don't procrastinate, hoping "it will all workout." It usually doesn't.

2. A leader should gather data systematically, give feedback, and follow a prescribed set of procedures.

3. Supplementary support systems such as counseling or drug clinics can help save valuable employees.

4. Termination should be done fairly but with compassion and help in outplacement when possible. Don't transfer "problems" to someone else's unit (with a glowing letter of recommendation).

SIT RIGHT DOWN: OPEN-DOOR POLICY

One important aspect of being a good leader is to be accessible. Subordinates should be able to observe what you do so you can serve as a role model. But they also need to feel they can talk to you. Personal contact can be crucial for morale and motivation.

The cartoon suggests that our leader has an "open-door policy" but that people must be cautious about interrupting him. In fact, this is just the type of message you don't want to send. If the door is going to be left open, then people need to feel comfortable about walking in.

An open-door policy can serve two important functions. First, being accessible provides an opportunity for employees to air their problems. In most organizations, managers are not covered by a labor agreement that ensures judicial due process. If people have a problem they need somewhere to go where they feel they will be heard, understood, and taken seriously. An "open-door policy" is often used to encourage such discussions.

For such a policy to work and to be used there are some necessary supporting conditions. People have to believe that their complaints can be anonymous if desired, that they have a right to appeal, that they are protected from retaliation, and that someone who is neutral or impartial may hear the case and make final judgments and settlements. These are the basic tenets of a just system of grievance. To expect someone who has a complaint about her boss to go to her boss and ask him or her to make impartial judgments is silly. They can't do it, they won't do it, and the system will crash. People need to feel safe if they are going to complain, and *you want to hear the complaints*. So build a system that encourages and protects the employee.

The second function of an "open-door policy" is to facilitate interaction and the exchange of ideas. It is important for leaders to know what their subordinates are thinking. Listening is a skill. It requires one to pay attention and to try to see the issue from another point of view. Dismissing or belittling others' ideas because they are different is a surefire way to get people to shut up. And besides hearing complaints, you want to hear the good things, and the new ideas. There are courses available for learning listening skills, and if this is a problem area then consider using them.

Combined with listening, the interaction provides the leader the opportunity to clarify issues, explain the rationale behind various policies and decisions, and distribute new information. On a more personal level, it allows the leader to deal with individual subordinates, become better acquainted with each of them, and understand their unique perspectives about their jobs.

Finally, having an open door and being accessible has a significant symbolic value. The message that you send is that you are available, you are interested in, and you care about your subordinates. It represents an organizational value that research shows is basic in companies where people like to work. If you expect and want your employees to be committed to the organization, then you have to reciprocate. One of the main ways to demonstrate that commitment is to listen to what they have to say.

Key Points to Remember

1. Open-door policies encourage people to bring in complaints. Knowing what is wrong in an organization may be more important than knowing what is right.

2. Any open-door system needs guarantees of fair treatment that are available in most systems of justice. People have to trust the leader or it will not work.

3. Being accessible also provides an opportunity to listen and learn what is happening with your subordinates. It shows that you care.

4. Accessibility also represents an important organizational value. It becomes part of the culture.

PART

VII

Developing a Career

I HATE TO THINK WHERE I'D BE TODAY IF I DIDN'T HAVE AN MBA.

DEVELOPING A CAREER

Frank thought he had it made when he received his MBA from P U. But, instead of a fast track to the top, he somehow got stuck on skid row. Yet, in Frank's mind his MBA degree has been valuable—maybe it gives him an edge in the status hierarchy of Hoboville. However, Ernie doesn't seem to be impressed.

Throughout this book we have seen Frank and Ernest in many job-related situations. Yet, like most of us, they do have a work career. A distinction can be made between a job and a career. The concept of a job focuses on aspects external to the individual; it can be described separately from the person. A career includes these external aspects as well as consideration of internal (to the individual) or subjective aspects such as a person's attitudes and self-concepts. Using these ideas, we can state that: *A career consists of the sequence of work-related roles, activities, and adventures that an individual experiences, perceives, and acts on during a lifetime.* A career can include many jobs and occupations. Frank's career development evidently stopped when he received his MBA. For most of us a career is a lifelong endeavor and requires substantial self-assessment and analysis and, in turn, provides many challenges and opportunities.

In career development seminars participants often write down the most important career issues, choices, or problems they are currently facing. Everybody seems to come up with a career problem. Test this on yourself. Take a few minutes to think about your current career issues. We will consider many of your issues in this section.

Why are career issues so important? A career represents a person's life in the work setting and, for most people, work is a primary factor in determining the overall quality of life. Our self-image and self-worth are greatly affected by perceptions of career success or failure. Career success is a primary symbol of social standing. It is an important source of feedback from the society in which we exist—an indicator that our life has been worthwhile and meaningful.

Charting a career is becoming increasingly complex. Individual careers are more flexible and varied than in the past. The image of going to work at 21 for life is no longer the typical pattern. Although some people do have a linear career path—moving up the hierarchy in a particular organization—most do not. Many more have spiral career patterns in which they move laterally and diagonally within a company or work for several organizations. Still others, like Frank and Ernest, have transitory career paths in which they move in and out of the labor force and between various jobs throughout their entire working (and non-working) lives.

In this section Frank and Ernest will help us look at some of the more important career issues by considering the following topics:

- No Working Parts: Self-management
- A Low Ceiling?: Career Planning
- Between a Clock and a Hard Place: Time Management
- Have a Nice Day!?: Stress Management
- Fire Alarm: Career Transitions
- What a Way to Go!: Retirement

NO WORKING PARTS: SELF-MANAGEMENT

In a sense we are all self-made. Although we are born into the world with different inherited characteristics and environmental surroundings, a good deal of what happens in our lives depends on personal effort. This is particularly true in the U.S. where we value individualism and self-determination. To his dismay, Frank found that becoming a self-made man does not come easy, it takes a lot of working parts and he wasn't quite up to the effort.

We live in a society in which a great variety of life-styles and work careers are realistically available. However, these opportunities are not automatically served up on a golden platter. No one plans and executes our lives and careers for us—it is expected that we will take individual responsibility. A key goal should be to ensure that everyone has an equal chance through education, health care, and other social services to take advantage of this potential.

One of the major concerns and reasons for dissent by students and workers against the governments of Eastern Europe and the Peoples Republic of China was the inability to control their own destinies. Typically, they were assigned to a school, to a given career, and then to a specific job, organization, and geographic region for their employment. Now that the limitations on individual choice and freedom are being lifted in the USSR and Eastern Europe, people have to make choices and take responsibility for their own lives and careers. The *Wall Street Journal* discussed the dilemmas facing members of the state sponsored circus in East Germany. For all of their working lives they had been controlled and supported by the state—a nice comfortable existence. Now they will have to sell their specialized skills in the labor marketplace, without any subsidies or guarantees. After more than 40 years of state direction and limited involvement in self-management, the prospects of freedom of choice and open competition can be frightening for many. Frank has learned the same lesson—it takes working parts to become a self-made person.

What do we mean by self-management? Self-management is accepting responsibility for managing one's own life, work-related activities, and career. It assumes that the individual has sufficient power and motivation to establish goals, develop and implement plans, and affect outcomes. The essence of self-management is the assumption of individual self-determination. It includes a number of specific components such as career planning and development, time management, and stress management. It involves self-renewal, change, and improvement—a never-ending process.

Most people do not pay sufficient attention to their own self-management. Managers and professionals spend much of their working lives planning, controlling, and directing their own organizations and the destinies of other people. Yet they rarely spend any time systematically thinking about self-management. If we are willing to let other organizations and people control our lives, so be it. However, if we want greater autonomy and self-determination, self-management is a vital process. Success is that point in life where preparation meets opportunity.

As a manager/leader of others, it is important to understand the concept of self-management. You probably desire individual autonomy, self-control, and responsibility. It is very likely that your subordinates want the same things in their work life. Current developments in human resource management suggest this. Concepts such as participation, job involvement, empowerment, autonomous work teams, and job enrichment all suggest greater self-management. The more people manage their own behavior while achieving results that are in line with organizational goals, the less need there is for rules and regulations (bureaucracy) or autocratic and coercive leadership styles.

This discussion of self-management should not delude us into a false sense of security in feeling that we can completely manage our lives. Many life and work-related events cannot be predicted. Luck has played a role in the success of many managers. We want to take advantage of and not be victims of chance. Self-management increases the probability that we can use luck and chance happenings positively. Good fortune in life seems to come most frequently to those who *position themselves* to take advantage of opportunities.

Key Points to Remember

1. A great variety of life styles and work careers are realistically available. Effective utilization of these opportunities requires self-management.

2. Pay more attention to your own self-management. No one can do it for you.

3. As a manager of others, recognize the importance of self-management for your subordinates.

4. Self-renewal is a vital part of the process and may involve developing new knowledge, skills, or attitudes.

5. Position yourself to take advantage of luck and unanticipated opportunities.

A LOW CEILING?: CAREER PLANNING

Living up to our potential should be one of life's major goals. Frank has a dilemma—he has achieved his potential and he is still a bum. Our destiny is not predetermined; we all influence our potential and how it is developed. This autonomy and empowerment to control our work and life is the essence of career planning.

Career planning is the development of a long-term and continuing process of managing one's life work. It involves setting goals and priorities, evaluating interests and abilities, considering alternative opportunities, obtaining resources to help in the process, and establishing specific strategies and tactics for career progress.

It is useful to think of *investing* your career in a work organization. It is often said that the largest investment most Americans make is in a home. This is incorrect; our major investment is in our career. The amount of money spent preparing for a useful and productive career is substantial. Lifetime earnings as a result of this career are even more significant. We should be a great deal more careful about this investment than any other.

The process of career planning offers many of the same advantages as do other forms of organizational and individual planning. Individuals who develop specific and workable plans are more likely to achieve their goals. Plans help them focus energies. They are less vulnerable to unpredictable obstacles and to having undesirable career decisions made for them by others. Career goals enhance motivation and performance. However, career planning does not guarantee the road to the top. Planning improves probabilities but does not ensure success.

Career planning need not be highly structured. It should be flexible and adapted to the individual. Obviously, the process may differ for the recent college graduate and the mid-career person. We should develop a career planning process that we feel comfortable with and will utilize. It is better to start early using a simple planning process than to wait until later when we can really engage in more comprehensive planning. It's possible that that time will never come and opportunities will be missed. Start the process now and we will become more effective as we gain experience.

With the idea of flexibility in mind, here are some suggested steps in the career planning process.

Start Now and Take Charge of the Process   No one has your own best interest more at heart than you.

Know Thyself   Take a personal skills inventory to determine strengths and weaknesses. Assess your values, beliefs, and life goals.

Analyze Career Opportunities   Investigate career alternatives. Look at various career paths and opportunities within your organization or elsewhere.

Establish Career Goals   Career goals should be measurable and should be both long and short term. Goals should stretch performance but be achievable.

Obtain Feedback   Develop your own measures of career performance. It is also important to have feedback from others—bosses, peers, subordinates—in the organization. A mentor can be helpful in providing feedback.

Manage Your Career   Career development is not a one-shot event, it should occur continually over our entire working life. It is useful to set aside a certain date each year to review past performance and to develop new career goals and plans.

This list suggests an overall strategy. There are many important tactics. For example, it is vital to maintain career and professional mobility. Don't be completely tied to a particular job, department, or organization. Try to develop a wide set of career options. As much as possible, choose your next superior—try to become a crucial subordinate to a successful and mobile superior. Be prepared to volunteer for challenging jobs and projects. Establish individual expertise and competence in a visible area/task. Try to change jobs, departments, or organizations at your own rather than others' convenience. Networking with colleagues and developing a mentoring relationship can be very important. Substantial research suggests that the career success of individuals is enhanced by an effective mentor-apprentice relationship.

Key Points to Remember

1. The number and variety of career opportunities create uncertainties and dilemmas for individuals in planning their work life.

2. Don't rely on others for your career development. You are the one making the largest investment in your career.

3. A career planning process should fit your personality and style. Start now and improve the process as you gain experience.

4. Make effective use of networking with colleagues and develop mentoring relationships.

5. Don't etch your plans in stone. Maintain a flexible set of career options.

BETWEEN A CLOCK AND A HARD PLACE: TIME MANAGEMENT

What time is it right now? How many watches, clocks, and other time devices do you have to adjust for daylight savings time? At least 3-4, or maybe even 10-20 (don't forget the car clock, the TV and VCR, microwave, computers, and calculators). Our lives are dominated by the clock. It is obvious that Frank is again not "in tune with the times." His Mickey Mouse watch has lost the hour hand and it apparently doesn't bother him much. He doesn't care whether or not the bus is on schedule—he can always catch the next one. This approach may have been appropriate for a rural America in the 19th century, but it is difficult to survive in a modern society without a better sense of time and some skills in time management.

Time is a unique resource. Everyone has an equal amount but it is not transferable, saleable, or salvageable. It is irretrievable. Time marches relentlessly on at the same pace, by second, minute, hour, day, week, year, and century. Time is not the variable; it is our perception and utilization of time that is important.

Time management is a vital aspect of career planning and self-management. It involves effective utilization of life's most important asset. It is not managing the clock but rather managing ourselves with respect to the clock.

Effective time management does not mean that we should be constant clock watchers and attempt to schedule every minute. Being a time-nut can become a fetish and wasteful in itself. It also does not mean that all of our time should be used working. Having enough R & R may be the most effective and efficient strategy over the long run. The key ideas of time management are: (1) to think more about how we want to use our time; (2) to work smarter but not longer and harder; (3) to do more of the things we really want to do; and (4) to enjoy our lives a good deal more.

Few people know how they actually utilize their time. Even fewer recognize the true costs of time spent on various activities. Other people and events make demands upon *our time*. The professor assigns a report, the boss delegates a project, and heavy traffic causes us to miss appointments. In effective time management, we are not just managing ourselves, we are also interacting with other people and events. That's what makes time management so important and yet so frustrating. We have the allocation problem of dealing with an inflexible and irretrievable resource. Time management is continuous throughout our lives. Unless, of course, we drop out, break our Mickey Mouse watch, and "let the world go by."

Time management is not a quick fix. It involves analysis, planning, implementation, and control. All of us can learn to be more effective managers of our time. Some suggested techniques are listed below:

- Make a list of your 10 most important life goals and prioritize them.
- Develop long-range goals and plans. Convert yearly plans into shorter project plans on a quarterly, monthly, or weekly basis.
- Make a time analysis. Diagnose how you spend your time. This can be ascertained by keeping a time diary over a period of two weeks.
- Compare actual utilization with how you want to spend time. Look for discrepancies.
- Establish meaningful priorities. Eliminate low priority activities, delegate if possible, reduce time wasters.
- Learn to say no. Do not agree to future activities unless you would be willing to do them today.
- Develop a daily to-do list. Prioritize this list and do the most important things first.
- Don't procrastinate. If it's important, do it now.
- Include slack time for handling emergencies/contingencies.
- Accumulate discretionary blocks of time to accomplish significant tasks.
- Avoid over commitment. This leads to rapid burnout. It is probably better to do a few things well than a lot of things half-way.
- Don't be a perfectionist. Demanding perfection often causes us not to start. Tolerate imperfections that can be refined and improved.

These guidelines are suggestions and not a panacea. Each of us should develop an approach to time management. Remember, the goal is not to save time—that can't be done, rather it is to do more of what we want and enjoy life more in the time we have.

Key Points to Remember

1. Treat time as a valued resource and precious commodity—it is life.
2. We cannot manage time or the clock. We can manage the effective utilization of our time.
3. Develop a life-long plan for time management.
4. Don't be a time nut who is dominated by the clock. Strive to be more effective (doing the right things) before worrying about being more efficient (doing things quickly).
5. Remember, time is ours but once. Waste it, and it is gone forever. Invest it, and reap the rewards. Develop personal guidelines for effective time management.

HAVE A NICE DAY!: STRESS MANAGEMENT

Frank is feeling stressed. He doesn't want the pressure of "striving" to have a nice day. He shares a feeling of millions of individuals. Increasing complexities and uncertainties in modern life lead to more stressful events. Mild stress is exhilarating and enhances performance. Excessive stress can lead to adverse consequences on our emotional and physical health, sense of well-being, and productivity. Like Frank, we may be stressed by seemingly inconsequential events.

Stress is an adaptive response, mediated by individual characteristics, that is a consequence of any external action, situation, or event that places excessive physical and/or psychological demands on a person. Job stressors are forces in the work environment that have the potential for causing stress.

Reactions to stressors are the result of evolution. Our cave-dwelling ancestors had two alternatives when facing a tiger. They could fight off the attacker or flee from the scene. The *fight-or-flight response* resulted in physiological changes such as increased heart rate, blood pressure, adrenalin levels, respiration rate, and blood flow to the muscles. Once the stressors were encountered, the stress response prepared the individual to either meet the challenge or run away. Fortunately (or perhaps unfortunately), today's world requires other types of responses. It is generally not acceptable to punch the boss in the nose; however, the human nervous system still responds in the same way. If there is a continuing series of stressors, the body remains in a stress alert or fight-or-flight stage, and can have detrimental effects.

Work stress is nearly epidemic in our factories, offices, and executive suites. People in other organizations—the social worker, inner-city school teacher, emergency room doctor, and air traffic controller are subject to excessive stress. Work stress is taking an increasing toll in derailed careers, broken families, alcohol and drug addiction, and other disorders. Work stress represents a high cost to society—some experts suggest $150-200 billion annually. Some work stress is inevitable and desirable. Moderate stress increases our alertness, motivation, and performance. On the other hand too much stress can result in loss of efficiency, poor performance, and adverse effects on mental and physical health. Too little stress leads to *rustout* with apathy and low performance. Too much stress leads to *burnout*. The key to stress management is finding the appropriate level where top performance and well-being are enhanced.

What are the consequences of work stress? *Physiological effects of stress* include headaches and backaches, heart disease, gastrointestinal disorders, skin conditions, arthritis, and other symptoms. The *psychological effects of stress* include anger, anxiety, depression, decreased motivation, low self-esteem, inability to concentrate, hypersensitivity to criticism, and a sense of alienation. The *behavioral effects of stress* include decreased performance, absenteeism and turnover, higher accident rates, alcohol/drug abuse, antisocial behavior, difficulties in communication, and withdrawal. The *organizational consequences of stress* include lower productivity, higher turnover, increased job dissatisfaction, and more dysfunctional conflicts. Stress may result in reduced decision-making effectiveness, difficulties with peers and superiors, and problems with subordinates.

The ultimate result of excessive work stress may be *job burnout*, a condition of emotional exhaustion, depersonalization, and feelings of low personal accomplishment. Job burnout seems to happen to the best and the brightest, the fast trackers who somehow become derailed. It is unlikely that we would accuse Frank and Ernest of having job burnout.

There are three basic ways of dealing with work stress: (1) treat the symptoms; (2) change or remove the stressors; or (3) initiate self-management of stress. Treating the symptoms helps individuals already suffering from stress. Individual counselling and drug/alcohol treatment programs are examples. The second strategy attacks the causes of stress by eliminating or changing the stressors such as reducing noise, pollution, and other physical stressors. Dealing with psychological and social stressors is more difficult. This may include the redesign of jobs, interpersonal skills training, team building, and other more general quality-of-work-life programs.

For the individual, the most important strategy is the self-management of stress. This approach makes the individual more resistant to stressors. Better nutrition, more exercise, effective time management, and relaxation, are examples. A key element is the development of strong social support systems. Ultimately, each of us needs to develop means for the self-management of stress. We should understand our limitations and the factors that are major stressors and recognize the early warning symptoms. It is easier to modify one's work and life style to prevent undue stress than to cure the adverse consequences.

Key Points to Remember

1. The goal is not the elimination of work stress but proper self-management at an appropriate level for high performance and satisfaction.

2. People who experience a large amount of work stress, who are high achievers, or who set unreasonable goals tend to be prime candidates for job burnout.

3. If you are in a stressful work situation or have a strong stress response, start your own program of stress management.

4. Monitor the situation and avoid unrealistic expectations and deadlines. Learn to limit exposure to stressors that trigger a strong response.

5. Cope with stress. Exercise, eat properly, avoid substance abuse, develop leisure interests, and clearly assess the demands you make on yourself.

6. If you are in a stressful work environment, consider specific programs such as meditation, relaxation response techniques, or biofeedback programs.

The Frank and Ernest Manager

FIRE ALARM: CAREER TRANSITIONS

Frank has cause for alarm. Most of us recognize the significance of the pink slip. Fired, canned, sacked, laid-off, terminated, severed, or made redundant all have the same outcome—unemployment and a major career transition.

Although the results are the same, there may be subtle differences. One departing employee made a cogent observation. "If I am fired, it is my fault. When I am laid-off, it is management's fault." Traditionally, managers and professionals thought that if they performed well, they would have job security. However, over the past several decades the situation has changed dramatically. Moves to increase competitiveness and reduce costs have led to massive staff reductions, particularly among middle managers. Flatter organizational structures means fewer top positions and promotional opportunities. Mergers and takeovers occur frequently upsetting careers.

It is obvious that being fired is a dramatic career transition. However, it is just one extreme. There are many others: promotion, demotion, geographic relocation, assignment to a new project or task force, interdepartmental transfers, job-change to another organization, second occupation, sabbatical leave, and retirement. We need a broad definition to encompass these events: A career transition is a significant change that occurs in a person's working life. It is a non-routine event that causes important re-evaluations and changes in attitudes and behaviors. It may be caused by external events or by the specific actions of the individual. It often means changing job content, skill requirements, responsibilities, power relationships, social interactions, and many other aspects of the individual's work life.

There are many positive as well as negative career transitions. One of the great joys in life is receiving a well-deserved promotion. Assignment to a ground-breaking project or task group can be rewarding. Many career changes offer new opportunities and challenges and provide an exhilarating zest to work life. Positive transitions provide feedback that we are valued by others.

There are patterns to career transitions. For example, young managers or professionals generally have flexible job situations and face many career transitions. They have typical problems—under-utilization of their potential, insufficient feedback on performance, political insensitivity and passivity, loyalty issues, ethical dilemmas, and mentoring relationships—as they find their way in the organization. Mid-career employees are generally less mobile and may face issues of plateauing and obsolescence. Major career transitions at this stage, such as layoff, can be devastating.

Dual career families face many difficult transitions. What happens when one member has an opportunity to move to a different geographic area for a significant advancement? Obviously, the decision to have children results in new career problems. Finding and affording suitable child care is a major issue for many working couples. Fortunately, more organizations are responding to these problems by having maternity leaves, daycare centers, and "mommy tracks."

Women on the whole face a somewhat different set of career opportunities, problems, and transitions than men. Many of these problems are associated with being a parent. There are a growing number of families in which the woman is the single head of the household and sole breadwinner. These women have even more career problems than dual-career families.

Many career transitions are brought about by external forces. We obtain additional education, change jobs, ask for a transfer, or move to different geographic regions. Many of these actions are voluntary. However, there are other cases when our attitudes, abilities, and behaviors cause problems. For example, poor job performance may lead to being fired—receiving a pink slip.

Research suggests some primary reasons why managers do not succeed; they include lack of knowledge and technical skills. However, lack of interpersonal and leadership skills do the most damage. Some of the most frequently cited reasons are: inability to get along with superiors, subordinates, and peers; failure to adapt to change; inability to adequately communicate; inability to work as a team member; becoming too involved in organizational politics; and failure to adjust managerial style to new circumstances.

There are many positive as well as negative career transitions. When interviewed, most people feel that they have had a good work life and have been able to make successful career transitions. Through more effective career planning and self-management we can make the best of positive opportunities. Again, success seems to come to those who have prepared for it.

Key Points to Remember

1. We all face major career transitions during our working lives. Some are predictable, many are not.

2. Some of these career transitions are externally caused and beyond our control. Others are due to changes within ourselves—our goals, attitudes, abilities, and motivations.

3. Learn to recognize the likely career problems and transitions during various career stages.

4. Be aware of different career issues and for men and women.

5. Maintain career flexibility and resilience.

6. Be willing to admit your own contributions to career transitions and to respond and learn from adversities.

WHAT A WAY TO GO!: RETIREMENT

Frank is already worried about retirement—particularly at the Ace Taxidermy Co. Being stuffed, mounted, and left in the office entry is not his idea of the way to go. Ultimately, the issue of retirement faces all of us. To the young college graduate the problems of the middle- and later-career employees—plateauing, obsolescence, demotion, forced exit, and retirement seem distant and vague. However, for millions of Americans these issues are very real. Just as the post-war baby boom has become the middle-age bulge, so will it become the senior-citizen tidal wave within the next two decades. With changing demographics and increasing longevity, more and more people will be facing retirement and 15-20 years of post-work life.

On the surface, a definition of retirement seems simple: *No longer working; having a life of leisure.* However, there is much more to it than this. In order to understand retirement it is necessary to put it in the context of a lifetime of work; it is just one of the career stages.

Working people typically move through four distinct career stages: establishment, advancement, maintenance, and withdrawal. The *establishment* stage is learning the ropes and job requirements, typically involving fairly routine work. The *advancement* stage offers new experiences—special projects and assignments, transfers, promotions, moves to other organizations, and upward mobility. Progression into the *maintenance* stage is often associated with difficult times. The mid-career and mid-life crisis is generally a period of re-evaluation, uncertainty, and anxiety. There is a gnawing feeling that life isn't turning out the way it was dreamed and that this is the last chance to take corrective action and change course.

The *withdrawal* stage generally begins when the person reaches age 55-60 and represents a gradual detachment from the job. The individual begins to look at end-of-career options such as retirement. This is another important career transition and may involve many opportunities and problems. The employee must think about substitutes for work as a major part of life, the potential loss of work associates and friends, and other changes. Individual adaptation may be positive—enjoying leisure, taking on a part-time job, helping others, voluntary activities, developing a hobby; or negative—apathy, indifference, dependence on others, and a sense of worthlessness.

The occupational career may be said to end with retirement. But retirement, like entry, is for many a slow transition. It is not a single event, it is a process. It can occur anytime over a 20-25 year period and it can be a gradual transition or an abrupt event. It is not necessarily a total severance from work and career activities. There is an increasing number of options available to people during this process.

National retirement policies are important to every worker, young or old. Demographic data indicates that after the year 2000 there will be many more retirement age people and fewer younger workers. Is it desirable to continue to terminate the work careers of an increasingly larger number of people at earlier ages? Retirement takes people from active contributors to inactive consumers. Can society afford this? Is this in the best interest of the individual worker? Research studies indicate that a high percentage of people who are facing retirement would like to continue to work in some capacity. Even with a secure pension, good health, hobbies, and other rewards for having done well, many retirees may regret that the primary symbol of their usefulness—a job and career—is gone. The pride and rewards from living by the work ethic is foreclosed to the retiree.

Traditionally, most companies have policies that support early retirement. Few provide encouragement for productive older employees to remain on the job. This strategy may be changing. Recent social security revisions provide incentives to remain at work. Enlightened companies are recognizing that older workers offer a potential choice for meeting their labor needs. A number of organizations have initiated programs that help extend the productive work life of employees and also improve their motivation and satisfaction. Such programs include: reduced-time jobs, flexible scheduling, job sharing, job redesign, job reassignment, outplacement programs, second-career training, recall of annuitants, sabbaticals, and phased retirement.

We are slowly developing more flexible approaches to retirement that give people a wide range of alternatives. Open-ended retirement options, with some people retiring at 60-65 and others working to 70 and beyond, are highly desirable for society and for individuals. Older people are being seen more often as potential resources rather than as a dependent population. The value of an individual worker should be judged on merit, not chronological age. It is in the employer's best interest to sustain the motivation and productivity of any employee who continues working.

Key Points to Remember

1. Retirement should not be thought of as a single event but as a process.
2. Retirement should always be a factor in career planning; it is of particular importance from mid-career on.
3. Continue to maintain career options. Recognize that new skills and retraining may be needed to cope with changing job requirements.
4. Organizations are slowly developing combined job/retirement strategies that provide incentives for people to work as long as they are productive.
5. Thoroughly explore all the options available for phased retirement. Let your boss know if you want to continue working.

PART

VIII

Contemporary Conundrums

CONTEMPORARY CONUNDRUMS

Fast and easy is the contemporary human approach to almost everything—fast foods, quick weight loss, instant wealth, and immediate success. Managers continue to look for quick fixes, and one easy way to organize or motivate or lead or control human endeavor. But, given the increasing complexity in modern society, there is no one best way. There is no set of steps to guaranteed success. Frank (page 103) has it down to two rules, but he is shrewd enough not to reveal rule number two—because it covers ''everything else'' and he really doesn't have all the recipes and prescriptions.

The fact that we have approached the subject of management in a light vein through the use of cartoons should not be misconstrued. The humorous touch is not meant to trivialize the message. Management is hard work—physically, mentally, and emotionally. Time and effort is positively correlated with success. It doesn't ensure it, but mental and physical effort that is applied at the right time and in the right way does increase the probability of success.

In this section we highlight a select few of the dilemmas and ''sticky wickets'' that confound the managerial task. Our aim is to illustrate how difficult the job can be. At the same time, we think that paying explicit attention to these basic issues can provide a solid foundation for success.

Personal ethics and corporate social responsibility have been the subject of debate for years. Some argue that enlightened self-interest is enough to govern the behavior of executives in modern organizations. Others say, ''No way, we need laws and regulations to ensure that the interests of all stakeholders—owners, employees, customers, suppliers, and the public—are reflected in the decisions and actions of any organization.''

Union relations—interactions involving collective groups—can also be a vexing problem. While industrial and trade unions have been losing members, teachers, nurses, and other professionals have become more militant in their collective actions. Labor-saving technology can eliminate onerous tasks and improve efficiency, but there can be negative ramifications. Making the best use of technology is a continuing challenge.

Can human beings continue to progress toward ''the good life'' and preserve (or even enhance) our environment? Economic viability may be threatened by the cost of clean air and water. Globalization challenges managers to work through the problems that are bound to occur—value differences, communication difficulties, unclear expectations, etc.—and to blend the best of various cultures and managerial styles in order to prosper. One final conundrum is diversity in the work force. Heterogeneity can be difficult but it also offers opportunities for new perspectives, creativity, and innovation. We will delve deeper into these issues by considering the following topics:

- The Bad Apple: Personal Ethics
- Institutional Shenanigans: Organizational Ethics
- And All for One: Union Relations
- So Long Pomeroy: Technological Imperative
- Our Next to Last Stand: Environmental Issues
- On The Move: Globalization
- He Is Different: Diversity

THE BAD APPLE: PERSONAL ETHICS

The drum beat of accusations, sensationalist stories, and actual admissions of personal wrongdoing has increased dramatically over the last ten years. Everywhere we look there is evidence of individual corruptness. Greed abounds—*Time Magazine* called the 1980s the decade of the pinstriped outlaw.

As the cartoon suggests it is hard to be wonderful on every attribute all the time. But that is not really what is hoped for now—those are *maximum* expectations. We would do significantly better even by meeting *minimum* standards of honesty, integrity, and trustworthiness.

The causes of the lack of ethical behavior on the part of some managers are complex. Obviously, personal upbringing, the organization culture, and the immediate situation all make a difference. However, there are some issues that can be discussed that focus on the development of character and personal integrity.

What we are talking about here are values. Values are the prescriptive rules of conduct by which we regulate our behavior. They are the oughts and the shoulds of our conscious mind. We strive to fulfill those values that are central to our character. Unfortunately, the values in America have changed some over the last fifty years and with respect to corrupt behavior in organizations these changes have not been good. Basically, three things have happened.

First, there is a pervasive attitude of ''me first'' and ''look out for number one.'' The shift is from a concern for one's community (colleagues, neighbors, family) to one's self. People are encouraged to always have a resumé out, to cover their backside, to maximize their impact and reward. The sense of service has diminished dramatically.

Second, there is a focus on the short term. The strategy is to take the payoff now—don't delay, for the goodies might be gone. This shortsighted perspective is behind many of the problems we see with respect to issues like safety and pollution. Take the profits now and don't worry about the future.

Third, the ends seem to justify the means. Everyone is focused on the outcome, not the process. We keep hearing phrases such as "at the end of the day" or "the bottom line." The experience of the event is also important and the means do matter. As one pundit put it: "We need to stop and smell the roses."

The combination of me first, get it now, and it doesn't matter how, leads us to what we call the Ethic of Personal Advantage. We believe it is these values that are the basis for the current level of corrupt practices.

What can be done about it? Well, changing values is a difficult process, especially when we are talking about the moral character of the population. Probably the most important change would involve the way values are learned and internalized. People need role models. If you see top level management being corrupt—and successful, why shouldn't you follow suit? If, on the other hand, management sets a good example, employees will pay attention and behave similarly. Socialization processes can emphasize norms of honesty and integrity. These values can be part of the culture.

But the issue is even broader than what one organization can do. The research on moral development suggests that higher levels of morality require that people be able to see issues from different perspectives, that they understand the complex consequences of their actions, and that they realize that questions of right and wrong often include the consideration of multiple—and maybe conflicting—values such as loyalty versus honesty.

What is needed is an institutional and educational system that recognizes these conflicts, points them out, and encourages people to reflect on them and discuss them. There are no simple answers. Changes in society's values will take a commitment on the part of educators, managers, and politicians. And changes need to be made in lots of areas. The next cartoon highlights some of the things that businesses can do.

Key Points to Remember

1. There is substantial evidence that corruptness is widespread and getting worse.

2. A basic cause of the problems stems from faulty values—values that reflect the Ethic of Personal Advantage.

3. Moral development requires an understanding of the complexity of moral issues and the opportunity to discuss and debate different points of view.

4. Significant changes are needed in our business and educational institutions to help educate and socialize people to have a greater sense of community and integrity.

INSTITUTIONAL SHENANIGANS: ORGANIZATIONAL ETHICS

What has been publicized as corrupt behavior has not been just a case of a few bad apples. One can hardly blame these incidents on the devious actions of misguided individuals. To some extent the norms of corruptness are *institutionalized*. They are accepted and in some cases even approved. Cover-ups, insider trading, the use of golden parachutes, greenmail, and other practices are wide spread and involve numerous people.

The cartoon depicts a concerted, team effort at corruption. These executives are acting in concert to defraud their stockholders. This type of activity suggests that we need to focus on more than just moral development to correct such problems. As we mentioned in the previous episode, a focus on organizational socialization and culture is important. Companies need to make it clear that honesty is important and that integrity is valued and rewarded. These values need to be held by everyone throughout the organization.

But actions are important as well. A system is needed where people can feel free to raise uncomfortable issues, to challenge what they think is wrong. Grievance systems need to be implemented that include basic guarantees. A person who grieves can remain anonymous. They should have access to outside counsel. They should have an impartial hearing and a judge (not their boss). They should have the right of appeal. And of major importance, they should have protection from retaliation.

Management-initiated grievance systems (MIGS) are usually lacking at least one of these protections. And they don't get used because of it. However, recent legal changes that protect whistleblowers have provided some support. The point is that organizations should be implementing these systems on their own and dealing with these problems internally. They should do it, not only because it is good business, but because it is the right thing to do.

A third set of activities involves the issue of responsibilities. As the law stands now, executives can hide behind the business judgement rule. This needs to change. People who engage in or facilitate or encourage corrupt behavior need to be held accountable for their actions. The legal climate is slowly imposing such constraints on management; but, again, such accountability should come from within, not outside.

The basic issue is one of social responsibility. It comes back to our discussion of community. Business organizations exist in a complex social and physical environment. There are many stakeholders besides stockholders. There are employee groups, the local community, customers, boards of directors and so on. Understanding that these groups have important needs and concerns should be recognized.

One approach has been to vary the composition of boards of directors. For example, Chrysler put a union executive on its board of directors. Other companies include people outside the firm from both the public and private sector. Such representation increases the chance that other constituents will be heard and research suggests that a more heterogeneous composition results in fewer law suits and less corruption.

So what is needed is a multi-faceted attack. Managers need to set the right tone in both their verbal message and their actual behavior. The culture and creed needs to emphasize and encourage integrity. Grievance systems need to protect people who report wrong doing. Boards of directors need to reflect different constituents. Such an approach can go a long way in fostering a more responsive and responsible set of individual and organizational values.

Key Points to Remember

1. A lot of current institutional corruption is due to acceptance and support of corrupt practices.
2. Changes are needed with respect to formal grievance systems and legal responsibility.
3. Organizations need to view their role as actors in a larger arena; one with multiple constituents with a variety of concerns.
4. Behavior that reflects honesty and integrity needs to be encouraged and rewarded.

AND ALL FOR ONE: UNION RELATIONS

"To join, or not to join?" That is the question for many contemporary workers. When is it useful to band together in pursuit of goals that improve the work life and general well-being of each individual in the group? Does collective action pay off? Or, is it better to negotiate a personal deal? If we choose collective action, who should we get as a bargaining agent? Apparently Frank was worried about this dilemma when he and Ernie were trying to organize the seven dwarfs.

At one time, the United Mine Workers might have been a good choice. Industrial unions—mine workers, auto workers, dock workers, etc.—have been powerful in the past. Another choice could be a trade union—pipefitters, electricians, carpenters, retail clerks, etc. Many workers belong to company unions that include a variety of skill categories.

Collective action has typically evolved as a defense against capricious and oppressive power on the part of owners. Unionization struggled until the 1930s when federal legislation guaranteed workers the right to organize without interference from employers. Substantial growth in the number of unions and their membership followed, with considerable impetus from World War II mobilization and continuing post-war growth in economic activity. In recent decades many industrial and trade unions have been losing members as the number of jobs in basic industries declines. Membership also declines when the union offers no advantages over what is provided by management. Decertification proceedings have had mixed results in recent years.

On the other hand, teachers, nurses, firefighters, pilots and other professionals have become more militant in their collective actions. This trend is particularly galling to many Americans because independence is so deeply ingrained in our national psyche. Some people believe unionization is bad per se because it its communistic; i.e., it emphasizes community and the common good. It might be expected (and even tolerated), they say, for people in overalls and blue collars because they are a little suspect anyway. But nice white collar workers or teachers or nurses or librarians or technicians don't need it and don't want it. The facts say otherwise. While membership in formal labor "unions" may have declined in recent years, the number and enthusiasm of workers in "associations" has increased dramatically. For example, one of the 5,000 teachers who rallied to protest during a 1990 meeting of the Education Commission of the States stated angrily to reporters: "I've taught for 23 years, and I've been nice for 20 of them, and I'm sick of it."

The assumption is often made that unions are interested only in more money. It is certainly important, but recent actions indicate that it is not the only issue. Teachers throughout the country have been more concerned about smaller class sizes in order to increase learning effectiveness. Nurses have bargained vehemently for more participation in patient care decisions in order to gain authority commensurate with their responsibility. Firefighters in one city voted overwhelmingly "no confidence" in their chief because of his "aggressive, fear-instilling management style, including retaliation against battalion chiefs for their union-organizing activities." Pilots, who in many cases have taken pay cuts in order to help struggling airlines survive, have collectively fought against management in an attempt to maintain safety standards that get short-circuited during cost cutting campaigns that often follow mergers and acquisitions. Inadequate, arbitrary, or non-existent grievance procedures also trigger sympathy and collective protests.

Enlightened managers in many of our most successful companies have abandoned the "us vs. them" syndrome and concentrated on the joint venture that is inherent in most economic activity. Profit sharing, gain sharing, stock ownership, and monetary rewards for innovative ideas are all ways of making partners out of traditional adversaries. Union leaders now sit on boards of directors. Enlightened union leaders also participate actively in designing organization improvement programs such as team building, quality circles, and action research—all focused on productivity as well as quality of work life. They have become less rigid by broadening job classifications and allowing cross training. The message is getting clearer; we can all benefit from making it a better place to work *and* learning to do the work better.

Key Points to Remember

1. Collectivism is a reaction to perceived systematic inequity or injustice in an organization or an industry that cannot be redressed individually.

2. Formal membership in traditional unions has decreased in recent years, but associations of white-collar and professional workers have become more prevalent and more militant.

3. A better educated workforce with high aspirations, different values, and questioning attitudes requires creative management responses.

4. When management maintains a dual focus on individual *and* organizational well-being, many of the reasons for unionization fall away.

5. Joint efforts to improve effectiveness and efficiency can be successful, and at the same time, increase participant satisfaction.

SO LONG POMEROY: TECHNOLOGICAL IMPERATIVE

Pomeroy is about to receive some bad news, he is being replaced by a robot. The technological imperative has found another victim. He is joining millions of other people who have found their work and lives affected by technological change.

Science and technology have become pervasive forces in modern society. The early industrial revolution was based primarily on the replacement of human energy with mechanical energy. The new industrial revolution involves automation and computerized information systems. Together science and technology are providing a new shape to the world. Technology is more than machines. It is the organization and application of knowledge for the achievement of practical purposes. It includes physical manifestations such as tools, machines, and computers, but also intellectual techniques and processes used in solving problems and obtaining desired outcomes.

A phenomenon of modern industrial society is the development of large-scale complex organizations for the accomplishment of specific purposes. These organizations are particularly adapted to complicated technologies. They have become the primary creators and users of technology. They are, in effect, social institutions for the utilization of knowledge.

There is concern that U.S. technological supremacy is fading. In automobiles, electronics, cameras, and other products we seem to be losing out. The Challenger disaster, the failure of the Hubble telescope, and other set-backs in the nation's space program have created doubts as to our scientific prowess. However, the U.S. still maintains an enviable position in generating innovations and we have technological leadership in many fields. We have fallen behind in some industries in the application and commercialization of these innovations. The Japanese have been particularly adept at using existing technology and applying it for commercial ventures. Americans want the big technological breakthrough and may neglect incremental changes. The Japanese seek *tiny improvements in a thousand places*. Certainly, it is important to maintain and improve our science and technology. Improving the educational system, continuing emphasis on R&D, better applications of technologies, and greater incentives for innovation are necessary.

For over three decades, writers have suggested that computers and information technology would revolutionize the practice of management and dramatically restructure organizations. These changes did not come with the development of earlier main-frame computers. However, after a long period of gestation, there is evidence that the revolution is underway, but not without difficulties. During the high growth periods of the 1960s and 1970s, the number of middle managers and staff specialists increased substantially. These people became collectors, processors, and interpreters of information—adding many layers to the organizational hierarchy. These middle management and staff positions have become vulnerable to computer technology. Many managers have shared Pomeroy's fate.

The large main-frame computers of the 1970s fit well with the traditional bureaucratic organization with a rigid hierarchy and centralization of authority and power. The newer desktop computers, individual workstations, and networking arrangements are better suited to more flexible, decentralized, and adaptive organizational systems of the 1990s. Network computing will allow managers to develop, use, and store information in an overall system. These systems can help people work together more collaboratively. The very shape of organizations and their managerial processes will be significantly altered by new technologies.

However, for most organizations this utopian dream of an integrated, computerized managerial information system is still in its infancy. Although computers certainly have increased the ability to accumulate, store, and process information they have not always had a positive effect on efficiency and productivity. Ultra-sophisticated computer technology that is not compatible with the needs of the organization and the capabilities of the people may actually reduce rather than increase performance. Pomeroy may be a victim of computer mania where the availability of a new technology is the imperative for change—change which may not be cost effective.

Technologies are not ends in themselves, they are the means to ends. They can be good or bad (nuclear energy or atomic bombs) depending on how they are applied. Computers and robots may have the potential for making the workplace more productive, but managers are in control of where and how to apply them. Making the best use of technologies will be an important managerial task in the future. The appropriate blending of technologies and humans into efficient and satisfying sociotechnical systems provides a continuing challenge.

Key Points to Remember

1. Science and technology are providing a new shape to human affairs.
2. Technology is more than machines and computers. It is the application of knowledge for practical purposes.
3. Computer technology is a major factor in reshaping organizations and can dramatically change managerial practices.
4. Technologies are means to ends rather than ends in themselves. They have to be used intelligently by people.
5. Managers face a continuing challenge in the effective utilization of technologies for more efficient and satisfying sociotechnical systems.

OUR NEXT TO LAST STAND: ENVIRONMENTAL ISSUES

General Custer's men would much prefer to have their engagement with Sitting Bull *not* be their last stand. So it is in the relationship between humans and Mother Earth. There is worldwide concern about the fragility of the earth and the feeling that we may indeed be waging a last stand against ecological disasters created by humans.

Let's face it, technological and economic advancements have meant increased exploitation of the earth's resources and a general degradation of the ecosystem. Prior to the industrial revolution people lived in relative harmony with their environments. Industrial advancement brought vastly increased use of all resources—coal, oil, and other fossil fuels; minerals, farmlands, and forests; and also created problems of pollution. Rather than living in harmony, the earth was something to be conquered, to be exploited. Chief Sealth of the Washington State Duwamish Indian Tribe in a 1855 letter to President Franklin Pierce said:

> "The white man...is a stranger who comes in the night and takes from the land whatever he needs. The earth is not his brother but his enemy, and when he has conquered it, he moves on...All things are connected. Whatever befalls the earth, befalls the sons of earth...Continue to contaminate your bed and you will one night suffocate in your own waste."

As the 1990s begin, world population has swelled to 5.2 billion and economic activity is expanding tremendously. A worldwide environmental dilemma is rapidly developing. The pressures for continued growth remain. Many poor countries still lack and desperately want the benefits of industrialization and economic development. How this dilemma is resolved is likely to dictate our planet's prospects for the future. Current trends suggest that there will be a doubling of the world population and a fivefold increase in economic activity by the middle of the 21st century. This could lead to unprecedented pollution, to global climate changes that would disrupt the ecosystem, and to the loss of a large share of the earth's living species. The need to balance economic growth with environmental preservation is evident. The quality of life for all humans is at stake.

The technological disasters of Three Mile Island in Pennsylvania, Chernobyl in Russia, Bhopal in India, and Exxon Valdez in Alaska are specific examples of fouling our own nest. Mankind has always had to cope with natural disasters such as floods, earthquakes, hurricanes, and droughts. However, toxic disasters are of a different order—they are caused by man's technology rather than by nature. They tend to create more fear and anger than natural disasters. There is also more awareness of the adverse impacts of the long-term and insidious environmental degradations—depletion of the rain forests; pollution of rivers, lakes, and oceans; air pollution; depletion of the ozone layer; and extinction of many living species.

When the first Earth Day was held on April 22, 1970 many viewed environmentalism as a nuisance and environmentalists as radicals who represented the political and social fringes. By Earth Day, 1990, environmental concerns had entered the mainstream of the world's political and economic activities. Living with and protecting the environment may be the biggest business issue. The 1990s could very well become known as the Earth Decade. Surveys indicate that maintaining the earth's ecosystem has become a major public concern. People are demanding more responsible public and private responses to environmental issues.

Eco-responsibility makes good business sense and more corporate leaders are making environmental considerations part of all their decisions. There has been a movement toward collaboration between businesses and environmentalists. One dramatic example of cooperation was the promulgation of the Valdez principles (named after the dramatic environmental tragedy of 1989). Developed by an ad hoc combination of institutional investors (controlling $150 billion of assets) and environmental groups, companies are encouraged to reduce waste, use resources prudently, market safe products, and take responsibility for environmental issues. The message that progressive companies are receiving is that eco-responsibility will be good business.

Managers are on the forefront of environmental issues. They make many decisions that have a direct impact on the ecosystem. They must deal with many difficult issues of balancing technological and economic factors with environmental considerations. Unlike General Custer, we may be given a second chance to save ourselves and the earth. Frank and Ernest, managers of the future, must remember that on a small planet, there is truly no place to hide themselves or their descendants from global environmental problems.

Key Points to Remember
1. Technological and economic advancements have meant increased utilization of the earth's resources and a degradation of the ecosystem.
2. Over the last two decades environmentalism has moved from the fringes to the mainstream of America's political and economic scene.
3. There is increasing collaboration between business and environmental groups and evidence that eco-responsibility makes good business sense.
4. Responsibility for the environment has become a worldwide concern.
5. The key issue as we approach the 21st century will be the integration of the desire for economic advancement and the need to protect and conserve the delicate ecosystem.

ON THE MOVE: GLOBALIZATION

Frank and Ernest find themselves in an unanticipated situation—they are working in the United States for a foreign-owned corporation. They are facing differences in organization culture and managerial styles and are having difficulty adjusting. Guaranteed life-time employment in a low-level job certainly doesn't appear to be to Frank's liking. Evidence suggests that this guarantee won't be in operation for more than a few days or weeks. After all, Frank didn't guarantee that he will work for Osaka Ultra Tech forever.

Let's face it, the U.S. and U.S.S.R. are not the big kids on the block that they were several decades ago, able to enforce their wills on other countries. The breaking up of the Soviet Block and the stumbling of their economies is apparent. Less evident, but equally important is the relative decline in the economic position of the United States. Rather than being the all-powerful economic influence in the world, we are now sharing this power with Japan, Germany and Western Europe, as well as Asia's four tigers—Hong Kong, Singapore, Taiwan, and Korea. This dramatic change should not be viewed as bad; rather, it is a reflection of the economic progress of other countries. It is unrealistic to expect that the U.S. could or should retain the military and economic power that it had in the early Post World War II Period. The rest of the world is accelerating, a "happening" to be welcomed rather than bemoaned.

Although the changes are inevitable, there are some disturbing sides to this transition. The huge increase in our imports from other countries has led to a continuing negative balance of trade. Even more disturbing has been the change in our international financial position. As recently as 1983, the United States was still the world's largest creditor nation with a surplus of $89 billion. Since then we have become the world's largest debtor nation with a net debt of over $700 billion. Americans have been on an 8-year binge of buying foreign products and services—a splurge financed by the national credit card. Someday soon the bill will come due.

The dollars that foreigners earn by selling us goods and services have been reinvested in a variety of U.S. assets—treasury bills, stocks, prime real estate, and businesses. As this trend continues, many more Americans will be working for foreign corporations. The title for the sequel to the Frank and Ernest Manager may very well be *The Hiroshi, Klaus, and Vladimir Managers.*

What is it like working for a foreign-owned company? Many Americans are finding out first hand—nearly 11% of U.S. manufacturing workers are employed by foreign-owned companies. Apparently, it isn't so bad. It may depend on which foreigners own the company. There are likely to be significant differences between British-owned Harper & Row Publishing in New York City and Japanese-owned Honda of America in Ohio. Perhaps the greatest current interest is with Japanese-owned companies. Most production workers find that the Japanese concern for human resources has created a favorable working climate. However, many managers and professionals working for Japanese companies find the situation less rewarding. These managers are concerned because they perceive that they have ill-defined authority and limited opportunity to participate in important decision making. A significant proportion of managers in Japanese firms feel that their career advancement opportunities are more limited. On the positive side, Japanese firms offer the advantage of greater job security. For Japanese managers the job is typically a larger part of life than for other nation's managers. Long hours and considerable time in rank are expected. Patience is a virtue. Americans are typically more individualistic and desirous of frequent feedback concerning performance. Even in an aura of enlightened human resource management there can be a clash of cultures and styles.

The rising amount of foreign direct investments and the increasing number of corporate alliances indicate many changes. The realities of the globalization of business suggest that workers and managers will become ever-more-multi-national. This again speaks to one of the most dominant trends apparent for future organizations. They will have a highly varied workforce. Future success will depend on the ability to understand and manage this diversity of human resources. (See *He Is Different: Diversity*).

These issues should be viewed as opportunities rather than just as problems. We have much to gain from more interaction with other people and cultures. We can learn about the management of human resources from different national perspectives. No longer are we the managerial elites of the world who can dispense knowledge from on high to developing countries. We should be engaged in more equal exchanges. This two-way process could be rewarding and may teach us that ''it is good to receive as well as give.''

Key Points to Remember

1. The United States is becoming less dominant worldwide in economic and political power.
2. We are moving away from concentrated and unilateral power relationships to more equal partnerships.
3. The trend toward greater foreign direct investments means that more workers will be employed by corporations owned and managed by foreigners.
4. There are pluses and minuses to working for a foreign corporation. There may be more stability and job security, but less participation in high-level decision making and fewer career opportunities.
5. These trends should be viewed as opportunities. The globalization of business and the effective use of diverse human resources will be key issues in the 21st century.

HE IS DIFFERENT: DIVERSITY

Sleeping inside the water bed in a wetsuit is a bit eccentric. Obviously, his wife is having difficulty coping with this strange behavior. Not everyone thinks or acts like us and they may seem to behave oddly. Traveling in foreign countries alerts us to many fascinating differences. But even within our own society and work organizations, there is an increasing number of people whose attitudes and behaviors are different. Differences are not necessarily bad. "Don't knock it if you haven't tried it." Sleeping inside a water bed may not be so bad after all.

We often view the United States as a melting pot where different nationalities and races are stirred together to create a puree—homogeneous people and a uniform culture. The "melting pot" concept was reinforced by public education and a common language. However, it was never fully effective—people from different backgrounds wanted to retain some of their cultural identity. Rather than a melting pot, the U.S. is really more of a "mosaic" society in which there are many different subcultures. Ideally, each piece of the mosaic contributes to the whole. In organizations, the maintenance of a mosaic human system composed of different subcultures is difficult. Integrating the efforts and interests of people and groups with different values and lifestyles taxes managerial skills.

White, older males working in higher-paying, skilled jobs and the professions; Blacks, Hispanics, and other minorities working on the farms and in lower-paying factory and service jobs; women as housewives or possibly as secretaries, teachers, or nurses—this was the natural order of things through the 1960s. But the civil rights and women's liberation movements and equal employment opportunity laws brought many changes. Organizations have a significantly more heterogeneous work force than in the past. But progress has been like a slow boat to China compared to what will happen in the future. As the saying goes, "You ain't seen nothin' yet."

The demographic facts are obvious. There will not be nearly enough native, white males to staff the labor force of the 1990s and beyond. Just 15 percent of the new workers by the year 2000 will be native white males. More than 60 percent of U.S. new workers will be women, and about 29 percent will be minorities. There will be a great deal of competition among companies for a more limited and highly diverse labor force. The companies that come out on top will be those that have learned to attract, train, manage, and keep the best workers from the rainbow of talent. Accepting a diverse work force and managing it for high productivity is an economic necessity—there are no other alternatives.

Managing diversity requires a different philosophy—it involves recognizing and valuing differences among people rather than fitting them into a common mold. It does not mean controlling or containing diversity; it means enabling every member of the work force to retain individual and group differences and yet to perform to his or her potential. Rather than emphasizing equal and uniform treatment for all, managing diversity requires treating people as individuals. The Golden Rule is not enough. We need to "do unto others as they would like to be done unto."

Learning to manage a diversified work force is not easy. Many companies are training managers and workers to be more tolerant of language and cultural differences, to identify and reject prejudices, and to be more accommodating to disadvantaged workers. Diversity-awareness training can help managers realize that their employees may not be like them or don't aspire to be like them. People are different and these differences need to be recognized and valued rather than disregarded or obliterated. Organizations need to understand their employees—in order to ascertain specific needs, satisfactions, and dissatisfactions. An open door policy, survey feedback, team building sessions, and/or group diversity awareness programs can be helpful in finding out how employees feel and think about their jobs.

Many of the new entrants will lack the necessary skills for top job performance. They may require language classes and training in basic math and computer skills. The Commission on the Skills of the American Workforce in its comprehensive study, *America's Choice: High Skills or Low Wages,* suggests that we have two alternatives. One is to downgrade skill requirements and lower wages. This approach, while possibly effective in the short run, would be disastrous over the long run. The alternative is to spend large amounts of money to train workers and upgrade skills. Companies need to accept greater responsibility for this training. Remember, however, that a skilled work force does not mean a uniform work force in values, attitudes, and behavior. A highly diverse labor force can also be highly skilled and actually add to effectiveness, creativity, and productivity.

In a country seeking to maintaining a competitive position in a global economy, the goal of managing diversity is to accept, incorporate, and empower the human talents of the most diverse nation on earth. Diversity is our reality. We also need to make it our strength.

Key Points to Remember

1. We are moving from the idea of our society as a melting pot to the concept of a mosaic where different subcultures can work and live together in harmony.

2. The makeup of the labor force is changing rapidly. There will be fewer white males and more minorities, women, and immigrants in the future.

3. Valuing diversity entails accepting, welcoming, and managing differences rather than seeking uniformity.

4. Diversity awareness training can help employees and managers understand and deal with differences in values, attitudes, and behavior.

5. The future labor force will require substantial training. Organizations should assume greater responsibility for developing a competent, high-performance workforce.

EPILOGUE

Is there a short story about management? Have we captured it in these cartoons and vignettes? Probably not. On the other hand, an 850-page tome probably wouldn't do it either. The body of knowledge about managing is huge, largely undigested, and ineffectively applied. We have a dilemma. Too short can lead to oversimplification and misapplication; too long can lead to overcomplication and inapplication.

Our approach in this book has been to try to make key ideas as simple as possible, but not too simple. Improvement may come through new values and attitudes, increased knowledge, or more skill. But the key is application. Many key notions about effective management are easy to say but tough to do. For example, *integrity*, the cornerstone of meaningful relationships, is elusive. *Clear expectations*, between individuals and organizations, take time and effort to establish and maintain. The *leadership* aspect of managing—providing vision, emphasizing continuous improvement, encouraging teamwork, and tapping latent human capability—is far more difficult than maintaining the status quo. *Eliciting and focusing effort* in new directions takes more energy than keeping the ball rolling. Providing *feedback*, particularly *positive reinforcement*, seems simple enough, but there appears to be a world-wide shortage of both. And, finally, who can argue against being *open-minded, aware of complexity,* and *tolerant of ambiguity and diversity* in modern organizations and societies? Yet these traits and behaviors are not widespread; they are much easier to write or talk about than to practice.

Frank has hit the nail on the head. Like most of us, he is looking for an easy route—some magic dust, the quick fix, a panacea—to success in life.

But managerial and organizational excellence doesn't come easy. If being adequate takes X amount of time and energy; being excellent takes 3X. Success often requires balanced emphasis. For example, Robert Blake and Jane Mouton stress the need for managers to have a *high concern for both* people and production. David Bowers and Stanley Seashore suggest that effective leaders emphasize individual support and teamwork *as well as* challenging goals and work facilitation. Victor Vroom and Philip Yetton argue that most managers would improve the quality and implementation of their decisions if they became *both* more autocratic and more participative—depending on the situation. John Kotter writes: ''The real challenge is to combine strong leadership and strong management and use each to balance the other.'' [''What Leaders Really Do,'' *Harvard Business Review*, May-June 1990, p.103] For change and renewal—both individual and organizational—the key is maintaining stability and continuity while, *at the same time*, encouraging adaptation and innovation.

A middle-of-the-road approach can be relatively easy and may lead to adequate performance. But excellence requires the more difficult and complex process of balanced emphasis. It is hard mental, physical, and emotional work, but the payoff in results and satisfaction can be exhilarating.

BIBLIOGRAPHY

Abramis, David, ''Fun at Work,'' *Laughing Matters*, Vol. 6, No. 3, pp. 93-101.

Cousins, Norman, *The Anatomy of an Illness*, Bantam Books, New York, 1979.

Cousins, Norman, ''Proving the Power of Laughter,'' *Psychology Today*, October 1989, pp. 22-25

Duncan, W. Jack, ''Humor in Management: Prospects for Administrative Practice and Research,'' *Academy of Management Review*, January 1982, pp. 136-142.

Harris, Sydney, *What's So Funny About Business*, Crisp Publications, Inc., Los Altos, CA, 1986.

Harrison, Roger, *The Cartoon*, Sage Publications, Beverly Hills, 1981.

Jones, Susan C., ''Using Humor as a Training Tool,'' *Training/HRD*, January 1981, p. 10

Kiechel, Walter, III, ''Executives Ought to Be Funnier,'' *Fortune*, December 12, 1983, pp. 205-206.

Malone, Paul B., III, ''Humor: A Double-Edged Tool for Today's Managers?'' *Academy of Management Review*, July 1980, pp. 357-360.

Wagner, Francis R., and H. Marshall Goldsmith, ''The Value of Humor in Teaching OB,'' *Exchange: The Organizational Behavior Teaching Journal*, Vol. VI, No. 3, pp. 12-17.

Please see page 125 for a cross referenced listing of Crisp Publications, Inc. Fifty-Minute Series titles appropriate to the individual topics covered in this book.

FIFTY-MINUTE SERIES BOOKS CROSS REFERENCE CHART FOR *THE FRANK AND ERNEST MANAGER*

PART I   GOING TO WORK
Interviewing: Preparing For Your Interview 033.7 $7.95
Entering: Your First Thirty Days on The Job 003.5 $7.95
Contracting: Personal Perfomance Contracts.............. 12.2 $7.95

PART II   WORK ORGANIZATIONS
Selection: High Performance Hiring 088.4 $7.95
Orientation: New Employee Orientation 46.7 $7.95

PART III   DOING THE WORK
Goal Setting: Successful Self-Management 26.2 $7.95
Motivation: An Honest Day's Work 39.4 $7.95
Rewards & Punishment: Increasing Employee Productivity . 10.8 $7.95
Performance Problems: Giving & Receiving Criticism 23.4 $7.95

PART IV   RELATING TO PEOPLE
Effective Communication: The Art of Communicating 45.9 $7.95
Participation & Feedback: Coaching & Counseling 68.8 $7.95
Creativity Creation: Creativity in Business............... 67.4 $7.95
Discrimination: Guide to Affirmative Action.............. 54.8 $7.95

PART V   BEING A MANAGER
Delegating: Delegating For Results 008.6 $7.95
Planning: Plan Your Work; Work Your Plan 078.7 $7.95
Performance Appraisal: Effective Performance Appraisals .. 11.4 $7.95

PART VI   BEING A LEADER
Followership: Learning to Lead 43.4 $7.95
Decision-Making: Systematic Problem-Solving
      and Decision-Making 63.2 $7.95

PART VII   DEVELOPING A CAREER
Career Planning: Career Discovery 07.6 $7.95
Time Management: Personal Time Management 22.4 $7.95
Stress Management: Mental Fitness 15.7 $7.95
Career Transitions: Plan B............................ 48.3 $7.95
Retirement: Comfort Zones* 73.4 $13.95

PART VII   CONTEMPORARY CONUNDRUMS
Organizational Ethics: Ethics in Business................ 69.6 $7.95
Diversity: Working Together 85.8 $7.95

NOTE: Order 5 or more titles and receive a 20% discount. Use the order form that follows this listing.

NOTE: Although not part of the Fifty-Minute Series, *Comfort Zones: A Practical Guide for Retirement Planning* is the number one selling title in retirement planning.

NOTES

NOTES

$$\boxed{\text{NOTES}}$$

NOTES

FOR OTHER FIFTY-MINUTE SELF-STUDY BOOKS
SEE ORDER FORM AT THE BACK OF THE BOOK.

ORDER FORM
THE FIFTY-MINUTE SERIES

Quantity	Title	Code #	Price	Amount
	MANAGEMENT TRAINING			
	Self-Managing Teams	00-0	$7.95	
	Delegating for Results	008-6	$7.95	
	Successful Negotiation — Revised	09-2	$7.95	
	Increasing Employee Productivity	10-8	$7.95	
	Personal Performance Contracts — Revised	12-2	$7.95	
	Team Building — Revised	16-5	$7.95	
	Effective Meeting Skills	33-5	$7.95	
	An Honest Day's Work: Motivating Employees	39-4	$7.95	
	Managing Disagreement Constructively	41-6	$7.95	
	Learning To Lead	43-4	$7.95	
	The Fifty-Minute Supervisor — 2/e	58-0	$7.95	
	Leadership Skills for Women	62-9	$7.95	
	Coaching & Counseling	68-8	$7.95	
	Ethics in Business	69-6	$7.95	
	Understanding Organizational Change	71-8	$7.95	
	Project Management	75-0	$7.95	
	Risk Taking	076-9	$7.95	
	Managing Organizational Change	80-7	$7.95	
	Working Together in a Multi-Cultural Organization	85-8	$7.95	
	Selecting And Working With Consultants	87-4	$7.95	
	Empowerment	096-5	$7.95	
	Managing for Commitment	099-X	$7.95	
	Rate Your Skills as a Manager	101-5	$7.95	
	PERSONNEL/HUMAN RESOURCES			
	Your First Thirty Days: A Professional Image in a New Job	003-5	$7.95	
	Office Management: A Guide to Productivity	005-1	$7.95	
	Men and Women: Partners at Work	009-4	$7.95	
	Effective Performance Appraisals — Revised	11-4	$7.95	
	Quality Interviewing — Revised	13-0	$7.95	
	Personal Counseling	14-9	$7.95	
	Giving and Receiving Criticism	023-X	$7.95	
	Attacking Absenteeism	042-6	$7.95	
	New Employee Orientation	46-7	$7.95	
	Professional Excellence for Secretaries	52-1	$7.95	
	Guide to Affirmative Action	54-8	$7.95	
	Writing a Human Resources Manual	70-X	$7.95	
	Downsizing Without Disaster	081-7	$7.95	
	Winning at Human Relations	86-6	$7.95	
	High Performance Hiring	088-4	$7.95	
	COMMUNICATIONS			
	Technical Writing in the Corporate World	004-3	$7.95	
	Effective Presentation Skills	24-6	$7.95	
	Better Business Writing — Revised	25-4	$7.95	

Quantity	Title	Code #	Price	Amount
	COMMUNICATIONS (continued)			
	The Business of Listening	34-3	$7.95	
	Writing Fitness	35-1	$7.95	
	The Art of Communicating	45-9	$7.95	
	Technical Presentation Skills	55-6	$7.95	
	Making Humor Work	61-0	$7.95	
	50 One Minute Tips to Better Communication	071-X	$7.95	
	Speed-Reading in Business	78-5	$7.95	
	Influencing Others	84-X	$7.95	
	PERSONAL IMPROVEMENT			
	Attitude: Your Most Priceless Possession — Revised	011-6	$7.95	
	Personal Time Management	22-X	$7.95	
	Successful Self-Management	26-2	$7.95	
	Business Etiquette And Professionalism	32-9	$7.95	
	Balancing Home & Career — Revised	35-3	$7.95	
	Developing Positive Assertiveness	38-6	$7.95	
	The Telephone and Time Management	53-X	$7.95	
	Memory Skills in Business	56-4	$7.95	
	Developing Self-Esteem	66-1	$7.95	
	Managing Personal Change	74-2	$7.95	
	Finding Your Purpose	072-8	$7.95	
	Concentration!	073-6	$7.95	
	Plan Your Work/Work Your Plan!	078-7	$7.95	
	Stop Procrastinating: Get To Work!	88-2	$7.95	
	12 Steps to Self-Improvement	102-3	$7.95	
	CREATIVITY			
	Systematic Problem Solving & Decision Making	63-7	$7.95	
	Creativity in Business	67-X	$7.95	
	Intuitive Decision Making	098-1	$7.95	
	TRAINING			
	Training Managers to Train	43-2	$7.95	
	Visual Aids in Business	77-7	$7.95	
	Developing Instructional Design	076-0	$7.95	
	Training Methods That Work	082-5	$7.95	
	WELLNESS			
	Mental Fitness: A Guide to Emotional Health	15-7	$7.95	
	Wellness in the Workplace	020-5	$7.95	
	Personal Wellness	21-3	$7.95	
	Preventing Job Burnout	23-8	$7.95	
	Job Performance and Chemical Dependency	27-0	$7.95	
	Overcoming Anxiety	29-9	$7.95	
	Productivity at the Workstation	41-8	$7.95	
	Healthy Strategies for Working Women	079-5	$7.95	
	CUSTOMER SERVICE/SALES TRAINING			
	Sales Training Basics — Revised	02-5	$7.95	
	Restaurant Server's Guide — Revised	08-4	$7.95	
	Effective Sales Management	31-0	$7.95	

Quantity	Title	Code #	Price	Amount
	CUSTOMER SERVICE/SALES TRAINING (continued)			
	Professional Selling	42-4	$7.95	
	Telemarketing Basics	60-2	$7.95	
	Telephone Courtesy & Customer Service — Revised	64-7	$7.95	
	Calming Upset Customers	65-3	$7.95	
	Quality at Work	72-6	$7.95	
	Managing Quality Customer Service	83-1	$7.95	
	Customer Satisfaction — Revised	84-1	$7.95	
	Quality Customer Service — Revised	95-5	$7.95	
	SMALL BUSINESS/FINANCIAL PLANNING			
	Consulting for Success	006-X	$7.95	
	Understanding Financial Statements	22-1	$7.95	
	Marketing Your Consulting or Professional Services	40-8	$7.95	
	Starting Your New Business	44-0	$7.95	
	Direct Mail Magic	075-2	$7.95	
	Credits & Collections	080-9	$7.95	
	Publicity Power	82-3	$7.95	
	Writing & Implementing Your Marketing Plan	083-3	$7.95	
	Personal Financial Fitness — Revised	89-0	$7.95	
	Financial Planning With Employee Benefits	90-4	$7.95	
	ADULT LITERACY/BASIC LEARNING			
	Returning to Learning: Getting Your G.E.D.	02-7	$7.95	
	Study Skills Strategies — Revised	05-X	$7.95	
	The College Experience	07-8	$7.95	
	Basic Business Math	24-8	$7.95	
	Becoming an Effective Tutor	28-0	$7.95	
	Reading Improvement	086-8	$7.95	
	Introduction to Microcomputers	087-6	$7.95	
	Clear Writing	094-9	$7.95	
	Building Blocks of Business Writing	095-7	$7.95	
	Language, Customs & Protocol	097-3	$7.95	
	CAREER BUILDING			
	Career Discovery	07-6	$7.95	
	Effective Networking	30-2	$7.95	
	Preparing for Your Interview	33-7	$7.95	
	Plan B: Protecting Your Career	48-3	$7.95	
	I Got The Job!	59-9	$7.95	
	Job Search That Works	105-8	$7.95	

Quantity	Title	Code#	Price	Amount
	For more copies of the Frank & Ernest Manager	077-9	$10.95	

NOTE: ORDERS TOTALING LESS THAN $25.00 MUST BE PREPAID

	Amount
Total Books	
Less Discount	
Total	
California Tax (California residents add 7%)	
Shipping	
TOTAL	

☐ Please send me a free Video Catalog.　　☐ Please add my name to your mailing list.

 ☐ Mastercard　　VISA ☐ VISA　　AMERICAN EXPRESS ☐ AMEX　　Exp. Date _____

Account No. _____　Name (as appears on card) _____

Ship to: _____　Bill to: _____

_____　_____

_____　_____

_____　_____

Phone number: _____　P.O. #: _____

**All orders of less than $25.00 must be prepaid. Bill to orders require a company P.O.#.
For more information, call (415) 949-4888 or FAX (415) 949-1610.**